T0246527

MAGIC CITY
ROCK

Spaces and Faces of Birmingham's Scene

BLAKE ELLS

THE
History
PRESS

Published by The History Press
Charleston, SC
www.historypress.com

First published 2020

Manufactured in the United States

ISBN 9781625858962

Library of Congress Control Number: 2019956037

For my friend Melissa—simultaneously the most Birmingham and the most punk rock woman I know.

CONTENTS

ACKNOWLEDGEMENTS

When you're writing acknowledgements for a first book, you feel the inherent desire to include every single name who supported you along the way. That's a bit different with the second book. Every close family member and friend who remained supportive along the way still deserves the same recognition, but by now, I feel confident that those people know who they are.

There are other names who came along who need to be noted, however, and several who were especially beneficial to this project.

Kristin Vines, who pushed this project to completion with immense support and proofreading when finishing seemed much too overwhelming.

Parker Storey, who I never knew I couldn't live without.

Alex Battito, who did plenty of proofreading during the early stages of this effort and offered many words of encouragement.

I am extremely grateful for every artist, club owner and promoter who is interviewed in these pages, but there are a few special notes:

Carole Griffin and Leif Bodarenko, who provided many of the photos in this book and are two of the kindest, most punk rock people I have ever had the honor of knowing.

Scott Register, who was always willing to talk and always willing to point me in the right direction.

Les Nuby and Duquette Johnston, who were also always very generous with their time.

Michael Shackelford, who was there on one of the first nights that I began trying to unpack what this story should look like.

Jason Hamric, who is one of the guys who helped build the scene a generation before me.

Layne Flournoy, who, like me, didn't grow up in Birmingham but has learned to call it home. I'm grateful for your friendship and everlasting support.

Roberta Caldwell and Pam Stallings, who have always helped fill in some blanks and have been two of the greatest champions of supporting live, original, local acts in the Magic City.

Josh Weichman provided many of the photographs in this book. I've long been in awe of his work, and I'm grateful for his contribution.

PREFACE

Birmingham's music history is long and rich. It's heavily rooted in jazz—greats like Sun Ra and Erskine Hawkins were Birmingham natives. Though her successes came after leaving the Magic City, Emmylou Harris was born in Birmingham. Though he, too, found his success after his departure, Gucci Mane spent his childhood in nearby Bessemer. For the past decade, Sara Evans has called Birmingham home.

It's been a diverse breeding ground for well-documented stories of jazz, blues, hip-hop, Americana and country. Birmingham is also home to the winners of the second and fifth seasons of *American Idol*, Ruben Studdard and Taylor Hicks.

But Birmingham's rock and punk scenes have quietly thrived for nearly fifty years. While it's been quite some time since Birmingham-bred artists have found mainstream Top 40 airplay, a community has been built that sustains itself—from the rock clubs that have come and gone to the Nick, which never will, to the bands that almost made it and the drummers who play in all of them at the same time.

It has relied on dedicated club owners who have always given local acts spaces to perform and independent promoters who have always found a way to host a rock show—be it in a dilapidated ballroom on the town's west side or the basement of a downtown church. It has relied on a radio station that—while it has moved dial positions several times over the last two decades—has maintained the curators who put the second-tier market on the map by breaking national acts like John Mayer, Matchbox Twenty and Train.

Heath Green. *Photo by Don Naman.*

The Brummies (formerly John and Jacob) in-store performance at Seasick Records. *Photo by Josh Weichman.*

Early St. Paul and the Broken Bones performance in Florence, Alabama. *Photo by Jesse Phillips.*

This is a version of that tale. It's about how all of those things have somehow come together over the past fifty years—the more mainstream, the more punk rock, the DIY spaces, the tireless promoters, the bands that almost were and the bands that occasionally broke through. It's about how all of those things have managed to coexist and find a unique identity in a city that was never known for its rock. It's not an encyclopedia; it's an overview with a narrative that draws a straight line from the origins of rock music in Birmingham to the current state of the scene.

1

BIRTH OF ROCK

While Birmingham has a rich blues history, and it has produced a wealth of talented singer-songwriters, it did not have much commercial success with original rock and pop music throughout the 1960s.

Marc Phillips began playing piano when he was eight. He spent his youth in Jasper, Alabama, and was part of several local bands before finally landing on the first Birmingham rock band to have real, national success.

He had been part of Rainwater, a band that formed with Tommy Calton at Walker College (now Bevill State Community College). Phillips moved to Birmingham after high school to find gigs. Walker County was a dry county at the time, and there were no bars or clubs to play there. Phillips and Calton wrote songs together and searched for other like-minded musicians with whom they could surround themselves. They were determined to land a record deal, and they were tired of playing covers.

Over the course of five to six years in the mid-1970s, Phillips and Calton homed in on the lineup that would be the best version of their band and worked diligently on perfecting their craft. The lineup that recorded was Mike Reid on guitar, Lee Bargeron on keys and guitar, George Creasman on bass and Michael Cadenhead on drums. That's the version of Hotel that recorded both full-length records. While the other players changed, Hotel's core always remained Phillips and Calton.

"Buddy Causey, who was kind of blue-eyed soul singer from here, told a guy that was working at Capitol Records about us and he came in from LA to hear us," Hotel lead singer Marc Phillips said. "He liked what he heard, and he actually quit his job with Capitol Records to become our producer and got us a deal with Mercury Records."

Hotel's first single, "You'll Love Again," was released in 1978. Mercury never called for a full-length album, just the single. That's when Tony Scotti of Scotti Bros. Records found the band by chance.

"[The single] was climbing up the *Billboard* charts at the time," Phillips said. "Our producer, Dain Eric, was on a plane with Tony—they just happened to be sitting by each other—and he was looking at a copy of *Billboard* magazine. He said, 'I really like this song by this band Hotel. Have you heard of this kind of thing?' And [Eric] said, 'Well, I'm their producer.' [Scotti] said, 'Well let me know if they ever get free. I want to sign them.'"

When Mercury passed on the full-length record, it let Hotel out of the contract. That's when Scotti Bros. signed the band. Scotti Bros. sold Hotel to MCA Records, which would go on to release the group's first two records: *Hotel* and *Half Moon Silver.*

Hotel's fit in the music community was always tricky. Though it was a southern band, it wasn't even remotely the southern rock that was popular across the region at the time. It wasn't Lynyrd Skynyrd or the Allman Brothers Band or the Marshall Tucker Band. It was power pop—progressive, as Phillips likes to call it. The band would go on tour with the likes of Toto, Hall & Oates and Little River Band throughout the '80s. "Lonesome Loser" by Little River Band was the number one song in the world on that last Hotel tour.

"We were beginning to sell a lot of tickets on the southern leg of that tour," Phillips said. "Little River Band decided to go up the East Coast and then out to LA. That's where their tour went. Sea Level, which was Chuck Leavell's band at the time, was supposed to be taking over the opening slot. Management approached us and asked if we'd like to continue up the East Coast and do Carnegie Hall. And we're like, 'Well…yeah.' They were going to can Sea Level and continue with us because we were beginning to sell tickets."

"You've Got Another Thing Coming" was beginning to see some chart success. Dick Clark had played it on *American Bandstand*, and Hotel was nearly a household name. It needed tour support to get to New York City, and that's when the label dropped the record.

"When that happened, we all thought to ourselves, 'Why is the label dropping us?'" said Phillips. "We have a song climbing up the charts. We are opening for the number one band in the world, and the label decides to drop the record. It didn't make sense to our manager, to us, not to radio, not to anyone in the industry. We found out we were dropped because we were having success. We were a tax write-off for MCA. They never wanted us to succeed. The more success that we had, the less attention and tour support they gave us. They needed a tax break. That, in a nutshell, is what happened to Hotel."

When they parted ways with MCA, Phillips and Calton worked quickly to form what would become Hotel's successor, Split the Dark. The group won

MTV's *Basement Tapes* in 1984. It performed showcases for fifteen labels and was turned down by all fifteen. It was then that Phillips turned his attention to production and his own solo endeavors.

Split the Dark, however, was the first outlet for Monroeville, Alabama native Damon Johnson. Johnson had his own success later in the '90s with Brother Cane before joining a later version of Alice Cooper's band, Thin Lizzy, and Black Star Riders.

"Damon was touring up around Geraldine with Pat Upton," Phillips said of discovering Johnson. "Pat Upton was the guy that wrote 'I Love You More Today Than Yesterday' [by Spiral Staircase]. Damon was his guitar player. I went up to see him, and I was blown away by his talent. We offered him a job with Split the Dark. We were trying to write new songs and feel our way through the '80s—the big hair thing and MTV—music was really changing. It was filled with a lot of one-hit wonders. We were trying to find our way through the synthesizers and synthetic drums and big hair. And Damon came on board and brought a real showman's edge to the band's sound and look."

Birmingham's rock and pop scenes were led by Hotel and Telluride in the '70s and '80s. These bands were often competing for the same audience but never thought of themselves as rivals.

"We supported each other," Telluride guitarist and vocalist Rick Carter said. "We still do. Music isn't sports; it shouldn't be competitive. Organically, I don't think people support that kind of competition."

Phillips and Calton produced a couple of projects for Telluride, and Phillips continues to produce for Rick Carter today.

"Marc is one of the most talented musicians I have ever known, so asking him to produce was a natural fit," Carter said. "And now that I'm working on solo albums, he was just my guy. He writes songs with me and plays on the records. It's something that's just grown over the past thirty-four years. I can't believe it's been thirty-four years."

Carter met Moose Harrell at the University of South Alabama in 1974. By 1975, Carter was playing in the house band at the Ramada Inn in Selma, Alabama, and the two made a promise to each other that one day they'd move to Birmingham and start a band. When Carter moved to Birmingham permanently in 1976, the two formed Telluride. By 1977, they had recruited Robert Churchill to play drums, Jim Liner for bass and Roger Bailey to play keys, and they were playing in front of audiences.

Telluride's eponymous debut EP was recorded by Decatur, Alabama native Johnny Sandlin (the Allman Brothers Band, Widespread Panic, Wet Willie, Col. Bruce Hampton and Aquarium Rescue Unit) and was self-released in 1980. Sandlin heard the band early on and had encouraged them to come to his studio and record when they were ready.

Telluride included the band's biggest hit, "Birmingham Tonight," a track written and performed by keyboardist Kevin Derryberry, who joined the band when Bailey departed. Carter knew Derryberry from the time they spent together in Selma.

The group's first full-length album, *Stand Alone*, was released in 1983. Its success secured major label support from RCA, and the single "Breaking Away" charted at number seventy-seven on Billboard.

The band stopped touring full time in 1998. After more than two decades of touring the Southeast, they had all begun other projects—for Carter, it was the immensely popular Rollin' in the Hay. Since then, they've reunited for several reunion shows across Alabama and the Gulf Coast.

When Telluride began, the club scene in Birmingham was still evolving. There weren't many places for rock bands to play original music.

"You had the Wooden Nickel and Old Town Music Hall, which came on a couple of years later," Carter said. "Really, that was about it. But you jump ahead now, and you have tons of venues. There was a lean period in there. We had a tight community in the '70s, and I think that has started to happen again."

"Birmingham has always been open to original music in certain venues," Carter said. "That part hasn't changed much if you know what venues are open to it. Original bands now have a better chance because there are more venues. Every brewery has a place to play music now. Draft beer was illegal in the state of Alabama in 1977."

Things have changed a lot. Hotel and Telluride were Birmingham's forefathers of making a living from rock and roll. With club payouts decreasing and music streaming increasing, it's become much more difficult to quit your day job.

"We didn't make a whole lot of money at first, but that's all we did," Carter said. "We made enough money to sustain life. Musicians today keep trying to do it full time, and some of them do. But for the most part, they're all making money as waiters. They're making music strictly because they love making music, and they probably play in four or five different bands. That was unheard of in my day. If you played in a band, that was the only band you played in. I do it, too, now. That's the way it works."

The roots that Hotel and Telluride laid in southern rock and pop in Birmingham quickly spread into other genres across the Magic City. Audiences began tuning their radios left of the dial to college radio stations, and nearby cities, like Athens, Georgia, were producing new music unlike anything anyone had heard. Alternative rock was emerging from acts like R.E.M. and Pylon, and new wave acts like B-52s were coming along for the ride. Magic City musicians were taking notice of the world around them, and the decades that followed saw Birmingham work to reinvent its own identity.

2

A MOVEMENT

O n April 18, 1992, thirty-five-year-old Benny Rembert was sleeping under the Twenty-Fourth Street viaduct at Morris Avenue. Three white young adults who had attended a party at Bill Riccio's compound stabbed the homeless man before dragging him to Railroad Reservation and leaving him to have his foot severed by a passing train. The assailants were convicted of murder and received sentences ranging from twenty-five years to life in prison.

"That's just another dead homeless black man, you know?" said Riccio, former Ku Klux Klan member and founder of the Aryan National Front, a Birmingham-based skinhead organization, on the 1993 HBO documentary *Skinheads USA.* "I wouldn't be proud of the fact that any of our members did it—if in fact they did do it. But neither do I feel any remorse because he's not my people. Here we have four, good white kids—that their entire life is messed up forever because of one homeless black man lay dead [*sic*]. And I think that's a tragic waste."

While HBO was filming the documentary, Riccio's compound was raided. He was convicted on weapons charges and served fifteen months at Three Rivers Federal Correctional Institute in Texas before returning to Birmingham to serve eight years of supervised probation. But his influence had already affected the ongoing struggle downtown.

Downtown Birmingham spent years trying to shed a violent reputation after the civil rights movement of the 1960s, and Rembert's murder was a seminal turning point. Once a burgeoning entertainment district, Morris

Avenue had already suffered immensely after the abduction and murder of a Chicago businessman who was leaving the Show Boat Lounge in 1977. Fifteen years later, a new generation was fed up and ready to reclaim the city that their parents had fled for the southern suburbs. The road to peace was still a long one, but the punk rock kids of Birmingham's Generation X were determined to find their way back downtown, and they laid the foundation for the city's twenty-first-century revival.

In 1978, Sam Ranelli and his son Frank purchased the Tuxedo Junction Ballroom in Ensley, a community on Birmingham's west side that had been among its most thriving and bustling throughout the early part of the twentieth century. This room was the namesake for the Erskine Hawkins jazz tune often covered by the likes of Glenn Miller.

The elder Ranelli had long had his eye on the space. For years, it sat mostly vacant under the ownership of a local dentist named Dr. Ellis. From 1964 until 1978, the once-vibrant space was used for storage. When Ellis passed away, Ranelli was able to persuade his estate to part with the property, indirectly leading to the gradual migration back downtown.

Cleve Eaton took over the property for a year or two. The Birmingham jazz legend momentarily reverted the space to a nightclub, bringing the likes of Count Basie to perform. But Eaton soon returned to the road with Basie, and the Ranellis reclaimed the space.

"Thurman Thomas came over and looked at the space and said, 'I wouldn't try to turn this back into a nightclub; I would rent this as an event center," Frank Ranelli said. "I can give you a list of social savings clubs and they would rent this by night."

The revolution wasn't televised.

The Ranellis purchased several eight-foot tables and chairs to accommodate the new groups that would be renting the facility. "I contacted one or two of those [clubs], and they started renting the place out," Frank said. "Once word got out, people came like crazy." And every group always left the space the way they found it.

Aspiring concert promoters soon figured out that they could host shows there. Few questions were asked, and much rock was made. Ranelli rented the space for $250 a night.

"I would tell them, 'Y'all come sign my contract, give me the money, I'll give you the key and I'll come back and see if you cleaned it up,'" Ranelli said.

The Beastie Boys played there. Propaghandi played there. Fugazi played there in 1991. That was the first show that musician and business owner Tom Bagby promoted; he was among the generation that led people back downtown.

Bagby said,

> *Downtown? That's where it was happening. The suburbs fucking suck if you're into different ideas. You get into art and you get into music and you have to come downtown to go to the record store and that's where you see the flyer. There's stifling boredom and neglect [in the suburbs]. You come to the city. If you're an artistic kid that wants to do stuff, you come downtown. The art is downtown. The food is downtown. In the suburbs, that's hidden, and that'll drive a kid crazy—not being able to express anything. Not having any peers. There were, like, four of us in my school that were into that shit. We'd find these kids at Berry [High School, in Hoover]. We'd find these kids at Homewood [High School]. "You're going downtown, too? That's awesome. Let's do this."*

Ken Sanderson sort of brought the scene with him from Auburn. He had successfully booked house shows in the college town, featuring acts like Green Day, and he had the blueprint for how to make things happen. He eventually left to found Prank Records—a punk and hardcore label—on the West Coast.

Sanderson passed "The Book"—a notebook filled with his contacts to book DIY—to Jennifer Chapman, and when Chapman also took off for California, she passed it on to Bagby.

The Birmingham scene had become a space where historic jazz nightclubs were hosting punk rock shows—a scene that somehow saw pop and southern rock acts like Hotel and Telluride coexist with punk rock and new wave acts like Jim Bob and the Leisure Suits and GNP (Grossest National Product). Everyone was in everyone else's band, and somehow everyone found a way—even if that meant sharing a bill.

The scene became a battleground between the group determined to move back downtown and Riccio's Aryan National Front. The punk and hardcore shows at local DIY spaces were often hijacked by the white supremacists, and Rembert's death was the beginning of the conflict's end.

Tim and Scott Boykin were born in Birmingham and returned after spending their teenage years in North Carolina. In 1982, Tim joined the Ether Dogs, one of the area's first punk bands (along with the likes of Jim Bob and the Leisure Suits and the HoHo Men), while Scott spent time in GNP. They regularly performed on Morris Avenue at clubs like Old Town Music Hall and the Cavern.

Tim wanted to start a band in North Carolina, but he had no platform. When the Boykins moved, he met the forefathers of Birmingham's scene—guys like Mats Roden, Ed Reynolds and Matt Kimbrell.

"When we got here, those guys were already doing the real deal, DIY all the way," Tim said. "They were already putting out their own stuff. There was a very populist attitude about it. People knew each other within the scene, and if you had something to contribute—if you could help keep the energy happening and keep things moving along—people would welcome you, whether they personally liked you or not. If somebody showed up and they had something going on, we needed them. They were doing stuff."

No one knew how to find their way, but they all worked together in hopes of unearthing Birmingham's forgotten potential. "We were just kicking around in the ruins of Birmingham," Tim said. "Downtown Birmingham now is this parade of wealth. Right now where all these lovely restaurants and bistros and craft beer spots are, we had empty buildings and stuff. And we were just running around in these empty buildings."

There were now-forgotten places like Bubba Town—a space atop Red Mountain in an abandoned television station. While it was abandoned, power had not been turned off. People would crawl through brush to the space with cases of beer and all of their gear because they had access to solitude in plain sight and electricity.

"Before anyone ever showed up there, someone had gone up there and graffitied 'Bubba Town,'" Tim said. "So it became known as Bubba Town. We'd have shows and parties up there."

In June 1983, the Ether Dogs, GNP and Jim Bob and the Leisure Suits performed a DIY show to benefit United Campuses Against Nuclear War at St. Andrew's Episcopal Church on Eleventh Avenue South. Shortly after that landmark show, Tim started Carnival Season with Brad Quinn, Mark Reynolds and Ed Reynolds. The band earned a development deal with MCA and achieved some level of international success. After recording some demos, MCA passed on signing the band. They shopped the demos to other labels before eventually landing on What Goes On from the United Kingdom.

Mats Roden (Jim Bob and the Leisure Suits, Primitons, Sugar LaLas) produced Carnival Season's first EP on What Goes On. The band's first full-length, *Waiting for No One*, was released in 1988. *Misguided Promise: Carnival Season Complete* was released much later, on Arena Rock Records. It included many of the unreleased demos recorded with MCA. Carnival Season split around 1989.

"I was a young person with a pretty severe drinking problem," Tim said. "We did this full tour around the states, and by the time we got back from that, I was really toxic. I wasn't functioning very well. That made things not function well with the band. We were shopping around, and I was meeting people from different labels, and I just got cynical about it all. I didn't like the scene. I quit Carnival Season because I viewed it as a band that was built to do that kind of work and at that time, I wanted to do something different."

Tim briefly joined Barking Tribe before starting Pinky the Stabber with Chris Hendrix. Tim began to realize the act had become too reliant on cover versions, and he wanted to refocus on his own songs. That was the birth of the Shame Idols, a band that signed to Frontier Records—the California label responsible for the Circle Jerks and Suicidal Tendencies. He is now part of Skeptic?.

A popular theory is that the Replacements named its fourth LP, *Tim*, after Boykin. Carnival Season had played shows with the Replacements, and the latter had taking a liking to the former. It would often publicly cite Carnival Season as a young band they were fond of, but Boykin neither confirms nor denies the theory.

3

JIM BOB AND THE LEISURE SUITS

Stuart is from Gadsden, Alabama, and he loves to play pinball—which is what he's doing right now at Brother's Music Hall in Birmingham, waiting for the Ramones to come onstage. As it is only 7:00 and he may have as much as three hours to kill, Stuart is not in a very good mood. For one thing, he is not thrilled at the prospect of an evening with the Ramones; he would much rather spend his money to see Bob Seger, appearing the following night at a new 20,000-seat coliseum.

Stuart is here at the insistence of his girlfriend, who is from Connecticut and a student at Birmingham-Southern College. (Stuart himself is indifferent to college, never having finished his first year at the University of Alabama in Birmingham.) He has longish brown hair and is wearing one of those baseball caps with a construction company logo one sees so many of in the south and southwest. He is also wearing a t-shirt that reads "Alabama—National Champs 1977." He listens to the Eagles, Doobie Brothers, Kansas, Ted Nugent, Foreigner, Pink Floyd and Journey. He hates and mistrusts new wave rock—"Why don't they just keep all that stuff up there where people like it?"—and is tired of hearing his girlfriend talk about it

And he is having a godawful time with the pinball machine. He is so absorbed he fails to notice that a tall, almost ridiculously gangly fellow in blue jeans and sneakers has been observing his technique.

"You hafta keep it out of the left lane," the stranger offers. "It looks like the same percentage shot as the right, but it's not. Real tricky."

The observer tucks his hands into his muff like sweater pockets. Stuart rolls up a fast 900 points. "You hafta work at it," the former continues, "keep it out of the left lane." "Uh huh," Stuart acknowledges, gaining 400 more, "think I got it." About a hundred points more ring up. "Thanks."

Joey Ramone turns and walks away.

—Allen Barra, "Sweet Home Alabama:
New Wave Meets Southern Hospitality,"
Trouser Press, *September 1981.*

Jim Bob and the Leisure Suits opened for the Ramones at Brothers Music Hall on March 31, 1980. Allen Barra's subject, Stuart from Gadsden, could have been anyone from Birmingham, really, but on that day, he was the kid who got a chance pinball lesson from a stranger named Joey Ramone. He wasn't familiar with the opening acts, but he liked them both. The club, however, closed within a year. Owned by Dan Nolen, it was the harbinger of what the Nick would become.

Matt Kimbrell, Craig Izard, Mats Roden and Leif Bodarenko were Jim Bob and the Leisure Suits, a punk rock band in the Heart of Dixie inspired by the sounds of the B-52s from Athens, Georgia. Kimbrell, Roden and Bodarenko met at the Alabama School of Fine Arts and began creating something that Birmingham had never really heard. This was the punk rock sound that would shape half of a blue-collar steel city's sound for the next two decades and beyond.

Kimbrell said to Barra in 1981, "We're fighting against inertia and this whole fuckin' city's idea of what's 'proper.' These kids go to these bars all the time, and they listen to the same boring boogie bands or country rock rehash bands. They're bored and unsatisfied, and they don't even know it. We get up there and play this totally different stuff that jolts them, makes them want to bounce, and they get pissed off at us 'cause it wakes them up a little bit. What we're singing about is what their lives are like, man, 'cause it's what our lives are about."

First Time, a four-song single pressed to 45, was released in 1980—the same year that Telluride released "Birmingham Tonight" and a year after Hotel debuted with "You've Got Another Thing Coming." If Birmingham had a sound at the end of the '70s, it was very digestible. It was radio friendly. It was pop rock.

After Jim Bob and the Leisure Suits, Birmingham no longer had one sound—it had two. There was the mainstream, and there was the

Jim Bob and the Leisure Suits *Photo by Leif Bodarenko.*

underground. There was a sound fit for a social, and there was something else entirely beginning to happen in basements, abandoned television stations, churches and the occasional club. But support from local clubs for original rock and roll was only beginning, as Nolen had begun shaping the forefather of Birmingham's DIY spaces at the Nick.

"They did good business," an anonymous Southside bar manager told Birmingham's *Kudzu* in July 1982. "But we got complaints from fraternities that thought the Jim Bob crowd was a little rough." Izard added, "That means that our fans like to get up and dance instead of just sitting and drinking beer." This is a struggle that still divides southern concert audiences nearly forty years later.

Jim Bob and the Leisure Suits struggled with its relationship with the Magic City. While Birmingham had grown to be a progressive southern city—relatively speaking—it still didn't have enough venues, and its limited radio stations didn't support the band's sound. At first, that was a challenge the band members felt tasked to overcome—not just on their own behalf but also for the sake of those who would follow and those who would never even create their own music.

"We have a clear sense of who we are and what our roots are," Izard told *Kudzu* in 1982. "It may sound strange, but the worse things seem to get, the more I think people around here need the kind of alternative we provide. I'm not sure we'd have that kind of feeling in New York."

The band's eponymous full-length debut was released on Polyester Records that year. Not long after the release, Izard left the band to focus his energy on his day job as an attorney. He was replaced by Charlie Muse. For a moment, however fleeting, the band's steadfast commitment to Birmingham waned.

By February 1983, Muse piled the band and its equipment into a Volkswagen and hit the road for New York City, stopping along the way for gigs in Athens, Georgia, and Greenville, South Carolina, to fund the trip. The group made $300 for a gig at the Mudd Club, one of New York's premier showcases of rising new wave talent. It was enough to pay for the band's gas back home.

On returning from the trip, Muse told *Kudzu* that the band was going to permanently relocate to New York City by September 1983.

"We could have played a lot of places roughly equivalent to the Wooden Nickel, and we would have been just another bar band that happened to be from Birmingham," Muse told Kathy Kemp. "But playing at the Mudd Club represents making ourselves legitimate. It's more of a showcase place,

Jim Bob and the Leisure Suits *Photo by Leif Bodarenko.*

where bands that are on the way up play. Performing for that crowd gives us credibility."

Just two months later, the band had a change of heart. Essentially announcing a farewell tour for the remaining dates that were mostly scheduled at the Wooden Nickel, Kimbrell told Bob Carlton of the *Birmingham News*, "I didn't think it would last this long, to tell you the truth. It started out as a joke and then it got serious. That's what happens."

The split was amicable, and it resulted in two separate bands: Roden and Bodarenko's Primitons and Kimbrell's HoHo Men. This marked another trend in the underground scene set by that quartet—each time one band has called it quits, at least two bands have risen from the ashes.

The first HoHo Men show was an accident on September 17, 1983. Jim Bob and the Leisure Suits had a show booked at St. Andrews Episcopal Church on Twelfth Street South near Glen Iris, but the band broke up before the show arrived.

"Matt called us—me and Walter [Kelley], who was my roommate—and said, 'Why don't we put together a band for this show and play the show? I don't want to cancel the gig," said drummer Ed Glaze. "That was how the HoHo Men started. We were still on speaking terms with Mats and Leif, but there was a brief moment there where Matt wasn't."

The scene became incestuous. A handful of punk bands had the same rotating handful of players as the end of Jim Bob and the Leisure Suits overlapped with the beginning of the Primitons and the HoHo Men. At one point, Glaze says, Roden filled in for Kimbrell in the HoHo Men while the latter was on tour with Tim Lee.

"I know it must have been really confusing for people going to shows, because they would come to hear the HoHo Men and it would look like the Primitons on stage," said Glaze. "Or vice versa. And we'd play a lot of dual shows at the Tavern or the Nick or wherever—Primitons and HoHo Men."

The common thread between every act among the group was the Velvet Underground. "I think we were the only six guys in town that adored the Velvet Underground at that time," Glaze joked.

4

THE PRIMITONS

Mats Roden and Leif Bodarenko recruited bassist Brad Dorset to play for the Primitons, a band hell-bent on doing what Jim Bob and the Leisure Suits never could: attaining national acclaim. Stefanie Truelove Wright was Roden's lyrical writing partner, though she didn't perform with the band. Quickly, the trio made its way to Winston-Salem, North Carolina, to record at Mitch Easter's Drive-In Studio. Easter, who was a member of Let's Active, had recorded R.E.M.'s *Chronic Town*, *Murmur* and *Reckoning*. The Primitons also enlisted the aid of R.E.M.'s early booking team Venture Booking.

"Singing was one of the casualties of the new wave, washed away by robotics, caterwauling and other noisy—albeit effective in the lungs of a John Lydon—attention getters," Claudia Perry wrote for the Richmond *Times-Dispatch* in October 1985. "New Southern bands—The dBs, Guadalcanal Diary, R.E.M., Swimming Pool Q's—have brought back songs worth listening to as opposed to music to be endured. Although it's unfair to lump the Primitons in with every other band from south of Virginia, the band does have one thing that links all of those bands—songs you can't forget."

The eponymous debut was released and distributed by Throbbing Lobster Records of Springfield, Massachusetts. The label had developed a reputation for releasing compilation records of emerging talent in the Northeast, and the Primitons was its first foray into the South.

And the Northeast noticed. "This debut disk from Alabama's best (ever?) band, sticks its head way the heck over the vast sticky wad of its collegiate-style cohabitants. When Mats Roden leans into those chords the way Bill Buckley leans into a stiff wind on the Chesapeake on 'All My Friends,' you'll swear the guy knows what he's doing," *Forced Exposure* printed in January 1986.

"At first glance, after a breeze through the enclosed bio, you fear yet another Southern (Birmingham, Alabama) band produced by Mitch Easter," *Gavin Report* published in September 1985. "Fear not. Whoever's doing the singing has a soothing effect. And the music, a collection of layered guitars and subtle acoustic pieces, steps out way beyond the R.E.M./Zeitgeist genre. This is the kind of record I'd search out from store to store if one hadn't graciously found its way to us via the mails."

Two tracks, "All My Friends" and "Stars"—a song that sampled "Stars Fell on Alabama" before sampling was a thing—gained traction at college radio stations across the country. "All My Friends" was especially popular.

"We were up at Mitch's studio and recorded ['All My Friends'] as an afterthought almost," Bodarenko said in the liner notes for the reissue, *Don't Go Away: Collected Works*. "It was brand new. We'd never played it live before. But we had enough time and enough tape, so we did it. I think we knocked it out in the second take."

"I remember writing the lyrics with Stefanie in 15 minutes," Roden then added. "It's really new wave to the hilt, but it's a glorious new wave."

The album broke into the U.S. Rock Independent Airplay chart at number twenty-two in November 1985, before climbing all the way to number seven by December. It was surrounded by the likes of Hüsker Dü, Black Flag and Dead Milkmen.

Brad Dorset left abruptly after the session with Easter wrapped, and Don Tinsley joined the band. The third Primitons player really became a revolving door—only Roden and Bodarenko remained constants. Tinsley had already played a bit of guitar and accordion with the band, and joining full time was a natural fit.

"I'd started as a bass player in bands in the '60s before switching to guitar in the early '70s," Tinsley said in the liner notes for *Don't Go Away: Collected Works*. "Mats and Leif told me they were planning to record a new album, and I couldn't think of anyone to suggest as a replacement, so I just did it myself."

That album, *Happy All the Time*, didn't receive the same critical acclaim. "We decided to produce the record ourselves, which in hindsight was something we maybe weren't quite prepared to do," Roden said in the liner notes of *Don't Go Away: Collected Works*. "Some of the people who had been working with us, such as our booking agent, didn't like the second record, so that was also a blow."

The record notably included a track called "Pope," which began to insert politics into what Roden was creating. It was still subtle, but it was important because the direction in which Roden was heading would flaunt his personal beliefs. Roden was no longer a player in Jim Bob and the Leisure Suits, the "joke band" that created a new Birmingham sound and lifestyle. He was becoming a voice for an entire community of southern-born outcasts.

> *And so the Primitons continue to live in Birmingham as local legends. Looking a bit like a psychedelic lumberjack, barrel chested Mats Roden has little in common with the tousled hair and boyish good looks of his partner Leif. "I'm never going to be on a major label," Mats concludes. "I'm too big, I'm too fat, I'm too ugly, I'm too intimidating."*
>
> *"I love to go around Birmingham with Mats because nobody knows what our relationship is," Stefanie relates amusedly. "And they don't know what he is. I always feel safe with him on dark streets."*
>
> *When Mats attended a tiny pro-choice rally organized to meet a massive anti-abortion rally in Birmingham, his commitment to the issue wasn't the only thing on his mind. "I did go to the rally and I did go to be on TV and I got on TV, OK," he explains with a smile. "I admit it. It was totally self-serving."*
>
> —Cream, *November 1987*

Carole Griffin had left Birmingham for Austin, then Europe, then Washington D.C., and then Europe again. She'd worked in bakeries, and she'd talked to friends about the possibility of one day opening her own.

"I always said I would never come back to Birmingham," Griffin said. "I paid a visit. I went to the Southside Festival and thought, 'Birmingham's a lot better than I remembered.' It was becoming a lot more cosmopolitan. So we came back here and opened [Continental Bakery] in 1984 or 1985."

She began playing in an all-female cover band called the Janes. Southeastern Attractions signed the act and began booking large parties. The Janes developed a huge local following, even though none of the women in the band had intentions of making it a job. Griffin, after all, had just opened her own business.

Griffin was in a couple of other short-lived projects, including the Lucky Bucks and the Ticks, but nothing had taken hold.

"I was eating lunch at UAB [University of Alabama at Birmingham] one day and I ran into Mats," said Griffin. "He asked, 'What the hell are you doing now? Why don't you come sing some backup vocals with me? We're in the studio right now.'"

It would have hypothetically been the Primitons third full-length release. "I started doing some recording with Mats," said Griffin. "I didn't realize that we were starting a band."

The Primitons called it quits in 1989, and Roden began writing new material that was nothing like either of his previous projects. "These new songs that Mats had been writing seemed like they needed to have a female voice," said Bodarenko. "So Carole was on our radar and we asked her if she wanted to start a band."

5
SUGAR LALAS

Mats Roden was a gay man in 1980s Birmingham, Alabama. He was a forefather of Birmingham's new sound—a punk rocker who started making music with friends and learned over the following decade that he had something important to say. Discovering how to say it was the challenge.

That discovery began one night at the Nick in 1989. The Primitons were still together, but Roden was beginning to realize his new direction as his friendship with Carole Griffin grew. And one night, Roden, Griffin and guitarist Davey Williams performed under the moniker Death in the Maiden.

Griffin said of the performance:

They hung three large pieces of white butcher paper. Art Price had done artwork on the paper. You'd pull one down and behind it was another piece of paper with a window and a design around the window. It was designed so Mats could sit behind the window and play Paul Simon's "I am a Rock." But he had on his Madonna outfit already, so he was in drag behind a sheet of paper singing "I am a Rock" through that window paper in the Nick while I was doing a trapeze act. On the floor beneath the trapeze there was Harper [a friend of the band]. *Harper was a country guy who knew something about everything. So, we put him in a tent—like a boy scout tent on the floor of the Nick with a microphone. Any time the music stopped playing, you could hear him talking. He'd be giving directions to Turkey Creek or something.*

Sugar LaLas. *Courtesy of Carole Griffin.*

I was wearing a mastectomy bra, men's gray underwear with fuzz on the front and torn leggings. Mats put on a wig and bustier. It was super fun and super funny. And it changed things for Mats. He quit trying to be cool and started being himself. He started writing music for me [to sing]. [While the Primitons were still together] *I said let's do Death in the Maiden. He came over to do that and something happened. He came out. Together, we were really able to be strong in bucking any kind of convention at all. He was an overweight, six-foot, 300-pound, Swedish, closeted gay man.*

The Primitons' sound began to change. It was always Roden and Bodarenko at its core, but with Griffin as a mouthpiece for Roden's lyrics, something entirely different was beginning. Bodarenko recruited Eric Onimus to play bass with him, Roden and Griffin. Bodarenko was keen to a band name with "la" or "la la," and Roden had devised several versions of a names with "sugar." The Sugar LaLas were born.

"We played together really well, me and Mats," Griffin said. "I was super innocent; he was super jaded. He wrote music and I performed the fuck out of it."

Roden's bandmates had known that he was gay, but it wasn't something that he paraded. This was Birmingham, Alabama, in 1989, after all. Attitudes were changing, thanks to acts like the B-52s in Athens, Georgia, but the HIV/AIDS crisis had reached its height in the United States, and fear continued to hold sway over understanding and education.

"We knew [that Roden was gay], but it was never anything we sat around and talked about until Sugar LaLas," said Bodarenko. "Then it became a tour de force. And it made us a little controversial. Locally, anyway. I can't think of any other bands that were onstage wearing motorcycle boots and a tutu."

Ed Glaze—who had been in the HoHo Men—joined the band as an additional percussionist, and David Kilmer joined on keys. The band's show grew to quite a spectacle. There were costumes and grand entrances. Once, Griffin insisted that the band carry her to the stage on top of a door that she had removed from her bathroom and discarded in her back yard. Another time, the band rode into the Nick on motorcycles. Mats was riding sidesaddle.

"The Sugar LaLas have earned a reputation for wild stage antics and hard hitting pop," the *Nashville Scene* published in September 1992. "Their show has critics scrambling for good adjectives. Words like 'psychedelic,' 'melodic' and 'intelligent' get tossed around like confetti in their reviews, but it's hard to verbalize the experience of seeing a band that crossdresses, brings its own

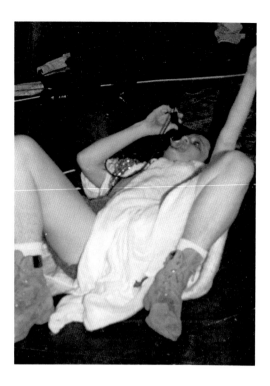

Carole Griffin performs with Sugar LaLas. *Courtesy of Carole Griffin.*

go-go dancers and usually begins its show by carrying voluptuous lead singer Carole Griffin onstage atop a makeshift Egyptian train."

"Mats liked being outrageous," said Bodarenko. "And Carole is so creative. She was really good at finding stuff at thrift stores and yard sales. Onc time she brought two trunks full of clothes and said, 'Y'all look through there and see if there's anything you can use. I got them for a few bucks.' There were some cool vests that looked like something a genie would wear, so I started wearing that with no shirt. There was a full gaucho outfit, and it just fit me."

"When me and Mats started dressing up, everyone started dressing up," Griffin said.

The band opened for the Smithereens, and within their first nine months of playing together, they went to South by Southwest. Of the set at the New South Music Showcase, *Billboard* proclaimed, "Among the acts that had people talking were the Sugar LaLas [who] take festive, colorful party pop to a new dimension."

They began playing similar showcases across the country and still didn't have a record of their own. "*Star Search* wanted us to perform, which was kind of a joke to us," said Bodarenko. "We considered it for a minute, but we ultimately decided that it might be the wrong thing to do."

All the while, Griffin ran Continental Bakery in Birmingham. "We would load in from Atlanta at two in the morning and I would come straight [to the bakery] and open at five [in the morning] with Vaseline caked in my eye," said Griffin.

Birmingham was supportive. The largest city in one of the most conservative states in America embraced the weird, sexual spectacle that Roden and Griffin had created. They packed every room the band played, from the Nick to Louie Louie's. James Beard–nominated chef Frank Stitt once hired the band to play a big anniversary party in the parking lot of Highlands Bar and Grill. He'd become a fan because Griffin baked the bread for his restaurant.

"We had young hipsters and we had affluent people you wouldn't think would come to our shows," said Bodarenko. "We had rockers and sororities and frats. It was a real phenomenon."

"We're shocked at our popularity in such a conservative town as Birmingham," Roden told *Continental Drift* in 1993. Asked if the Sugar LaLas were a release for the community, he replied, "Definitely for us. I don't know about the community."

The group signed a publishing deal with Peermusic, a move that Roden and Bodarenko insisted on. The two veterans believed that inking a publishing deal before a record deal was in the band's best interest.

"We got a bunch of money because those major, major labels [including MCA] were courting us," said Griffin. "We started doing demos and traveling a lot, but Mats was agoraphobic so he'd have to bring his mattress in the van. He couldn't stay anywhere overnight, so we'd have to come home every night, which pissed me off because I had to be the designated driver, and I'd wear a crash helmet in the van because I was sure we would have an accident. Mats would get unstable when I'd drive. He'd yell and kick the seats and after a while, I wearied of the whole thing—it got to where it wasn't as fun anymore."

Roden recalled the band's final days with Griffin in *Magic City Nights: Birmingham's Rock and Roll Years*:

> We developed an act, as it were, at The Nick. It then solidified when we went to South by Southwest in Austin and played a showcase there. We had a lot of response there from publishers and record labels, and so we really got into this hardcore gang trying to get a deal playing all these showcases all over the country: New York, Austin, Nashville and Atlanta. We played every showcase we could. We took the whole act, dancers and all—it was

This page and opposite: Sugar LaLas. *Courtesy of Carole Griffin.*

really a nightmare in a way. We ended up getting a publishing deal, and we had a huge bidding war. I am embarrassed to say, but it was over the band between six or seven publishers. It was all predicated on these tunes that I had written, and so I signed them away for the band. Then it just deteriorated for Carole and I and for the rest of the band. We were really just burned out at this point because we had spent a lot of time working toward these goals. Our personal relationship as well as our professional relationship just really suffered. That is just the way a lot of bands go. It just wears you out. Especially what we were doing, which was exhausting but it was really fun. It was a lot of fun for me, but she split just after six months of the signing of the contract. That was really devastating for me and the band. It just left things really screwed up.

Griffin walked away from Sugar LaLas on the cusp of stardom. The band that she left behind tried hard to replace her but never could.

"All the girls that we auditioned—there was one girl that we used for a few gigs—but the vibe wasn't right," said Bodarenko. "We couldn't match the vibe we had when Carole was in the band. So I left. Because I realized it was never gonna be as good as when Carole was in the band."

They settled on Lisa Engelken, who has since had a successful career as a jazz vocalist.

Roden never let the dream die. For a full year, until his death from complications due to a stroke in 2014, he was still working on new material that should have been performed by the Sugar LaLas—material that he hoped someone would perform. After his stroke, he could no longer play guitar, so he taught Les Nuby at Ol Elegante recording studio how to play his parts.

"I was playing guitar and drums and Daniel Farris was engineering and we were getting a female vocalist to come in and sing," said Nuby. "He never lost the dream that it could work. Even if it meant that he wasn't on tour and he could sell the songs and somebody else could play them."

Nuby had a successful career as part of Verbena with Scott Bondy, Duquette Johnston and Griffin's sister, Anne-Marie. And while things weren't always great, he reflects on the overall experience as a positive one. "Sure, there's the 'Let me tell you the horror story of when we were all hated each other in Minneapolis,'" said Nuby. "But stories like that don't matter. Everybody gets on tour and gets mad at each other. But true tragedy might be that Sugar LaLas story. I've always wondered why Carole walked away from it. Her dream in life was to open Continental Bakery, and it all worked."

6

VERBENA

Anne-Marie Griffin sounded a lot like her older sister, Carole, but Sugar LaLas never tried to recruit her as a replacement because she had already begun doing her own thing.

"She was in a little shoegazer band at the time," said Glaze, percussionist for the Sugar LaLas. "We had this practice space at Twentieth Street and Eighth [University] Avenue [approximately the current location of the Residence Inn by Marriott]. It was this big, vacant office building. Remy Zero had the space at the end of the hall; we were close to the front. And her band was practicing down there, too. They were loud as hell, man. Their room was a third our size, and they practiced twice as loud. I don't know how they lived through it."

Before people and business began moving back downtown, there was a lot of vacant space. Developers and landlords had a difficult time finding occupants for the space, so it was cheap. And that office space became ground zero for the developing '90s rock scene. Multiple bands of all genres used the vacated offices just off of UAB's campus as practice space.

"They couldn't really rent it out," said Glaze, "and I think they got wind of, 'Hey, there's a bunch of bands that need electricity. It worked out great until some of the folks—some folks didn't respect the property—and they ended up blowing it for everybody."

Les Nuby and Scott (now A.A.) Bondy were attending Mountain Brook High School when they formed Volume in the early '90s. Bondy had already been playing with Daniel (now Duquette) Johnston and with drummer Carson Lamm.

"We recorded Volume demos at Bates Brothers in Hueytown," said Johnston. "When we went out there, they were doing nothing but Christian music. We were a bunch of crazy teenagers on acid. We used my nephew's name on the cassettes as our 'manager' and used my phone number and sent it to indie labels. [The scheme gave us an opportunity to] play a showcase in Atlanta."

The boys of Volume spent their free time tuning guitars for Sugar LaLas because they were underage, and it was the only way they could get into Sugar LaLas shows.

"I was hanging out a bunch with Anne-Marie and Carole and listening to them sing, and I wanted to do something with Anne-Marie because I came from a rootsier background," said Johnston. "I was into Gram Parsons and the Dead. I introduced Bondy to her and it worked."

Anne-Marie—eleven years Carole's junior—started playing guitar for what was still called Volume until Nuby decided to leave, and the band became known as Shallow.

"We grew up in a really musical family," said Anne-Marie. "We all took music lessons growing up and it was just part of the family environment. I was around during the Sugar LaLas, and she introduced me to Scott and Daniel."

She was twenty years old or so when they all began regularly attending her older sister's shows. Carole gave Anne-Marie her first electric guitar.

"Kerry Echols [of the *Black & White*] took an interest in us and started sending our music to publicists that he knew," Anne-Marie said. "Before we knew it, we were getting contacted by labels. People were flying in to see us at the Nick. And that's when I realized, 'We're probably gonna get a record deal.' That's when it became serious. I was in college at the time. I really didn't think it would become anything, but it did."

"I was none too pleased to be leaving my high school band because Scott wanted to be in a band with his girlfriend," said Nuby, as Scott and Anne-Marie had become romantically involved at that point as well. "But I wasn't stupid. It was *really* good. Their voices had always sounded amazing together. So I was like, 'Okay, I get it. It's a lot cooler; you want to go in a different direction."

Another year passed, and Lamm left the band. Nuby reemerged as the drummer. "I was like, 'Oh, sure, you guys need a drummer,'" said Nuby, "and we didn't know any, so I said, 'Sure, I'll sit in, it'll be fun.' And then twelve years went by."

When Nuby came back to the band, the sound began to change drastically. Shallow had a shoegaze vibe, but this band was much heavier.

Another band existed that called itself Shallow, so it was understood that if this Birmingham band had any real success, the name of the band would need change.

"We were getting more [Rolling] Stones sounding—there was more swagger," Johnston said. "Bondy was developing as a songwriter, and Les was a ferocious drummer. That's why it fit with him on drums."

"The first show that I played with them was at the Nick," Nuby said, "and it was like, 'Oh yeah, we're called Verbena now.' And I remember there not being much discussion about it. It was just like, 'Alright. Here we go!'"

Verbena, as it became known, made the trek to South by Southwest and was discovered by the team at Merge Records. "Kerry Echols stopped us from signing bad publishing deals when we were young and dumb," said Johnston. "You want to sign deals and make money. That's when Merge came along."

Anne-Marie was the negotiator—very careful and skeptical of the band's business dealings. But her acumen didn't come from watching the rise and fall of Sugar LaLas. She'd read *Mansion on the Hill: Dylan, Young, Geffen, Springsteen and the Head-On Collision of Rock and Commerce* by Fred Goodman, and it shaped the way she would approach everything that the band did.

"Anne-Marie was brilliant with all of the business stuff," said Johnston. "We would sit in meetings and toss questions at label execs like, 'How much can we recoup and how much can we not?'"

Merge Records had already decided to release a single before Nuby returned, but at that time, it had not committed to a full-length album. Setanta Records in the United Kingdom first distributed the debut, *Souls for Sale*, in 1997, and Merge signed an agreement to distribute the record stateside. The album was produced by Dave Fridmann, notably known for his work with Weezer and the Flaming Lips, at Sweetfish in Upstate New York.

"Anne-Marie had a credit card, and we would book these four- to six-week tours playing anywhere," said Nuby. "We'd play at the Nick in every town and occasionally have a cool show in Chicago or wherever. Then we'd come back home and play a bigger show at Zydeco or the Nick, pay off the credit card and go back out."

That's when people began finding Verbena. First it was Veruca Salt drummer Jim Shapiro. He shared the group's music with Veruca Salt singer Louise Post, who shared the music with her boyfriend Dave Grohl.

"Dave heard the first Verbena record and wanted us to go out and play some shows with [Foo Fighters]," said Nuby. "But we had already signed to do a couple of records with Capitol Records. Foo Fighters weren't huge at the time; their second record hadn't come out. It was, 'Oh yeah, that band that Dave Grohl is the guitarist and lead singer of wants us to come out. That could be fun.'"

Verbena toured the United States with Foo Fighters for a couple of weeks before heading out on a previously planned United States tour with Jesus Lizard for two more weeks. Then, Foo Fighters asked the group to join their European tour in England, Spain, France and Italy.

"We were on tour with Foo Fighters when my daughter was born," said Johnston. "I drove back from Charlotte and got here one hour before she was born. It was an eight-hour drive through tornadoes, and I listened to *Loveless* by My Bloody Valentine for the entire eight hours. If you've not sold as many records as Foo Fighters, you don't have room to be an arrogant prick. Those guys have sold millions, and they treated us like family. Everything that we didn't get for our kid on our baby registry, Foo Fighters bought for us."

Grohl produced Verbena's major label debut *Into the Pink*, which was distributed by Capitol in 1999. Johnston left the band a week before recording began. The sophomore release was recorded as a trio: Bondy, Griffin and Nuby. Griffin briefly played bass in Johnston's absence.

"There was stuff going on with folks in the band," Johnston said. "I had a kid. I wanted to play in Whiskeytown. Ryan [Adams] was a huge Verbena fan, and I was a huge Whiskeytown fan. If I was gonna go play with someone else, that was it. Whiskeytown disbanded just before we were going to make it happen."

Johnston had met Adams in Austin, Texas, when Verbena was opening for Spoon. They bonded over their shared love of the Grateful Dead. No one else in either of their bands was into the music.

While touring in support of *Into the Pink*, the band hired former Weezer bassist Mikey Welsh as the touring bassist, allowing Griffin to return to rhythm guitar. Griffin eventually left the band, which then hired Galen Polivka [now of the Hold Steady] as the touring bassist for a year.

After a period of uncertainty, Nuby and Bondy brought Nick Daviston on board to play bass, and Taylor Hollingsworth toured on rhythm guitar. The group recorded one more record, *La Musica Negra*, in 2003.

"We didn't stop," said Nuby. "Maybe we should have. The band definitely changed. It changed in a way that was more centric on Scott, vocally. But he rose to the challenge and wrote songs where, 'Okay, now there's one primary vocalist instead of harmonies.' Honestly, it became more rock. The album we did with Grohl was pretty straightforward rock music, but the third album was more Zeppelin influenced."

The band finished that album cycle and had begun preproduction on a fourth record. Bondy had started recording another album with Nuby when they were dropped—an endgame that they had quietly sought. Those recordings became the demos for the A.A. Body solo debut *American Hearts*, released in 2007.

"I don't know if we've ever *called* it quits," said Nuby. "In 2004—thirteen years ago—we hadn't really done anything in a year. Scott decided to move to Upstate New York to live with some friends. I had been living in L.A., but I moved back to Birmingham after I ended a relationship. Nick and his wife had twins. At that point, Scott and I had a conversation where we asked each other, 'What do we do? Do we get another bass player? Do we take a break?' We agreed to take a break. We played one last show around the holidays as a three piece, with me and Scott and Nick."

Johnston created a project called CutGrass and played with the Rebel Kings. He released his solo debut, *Etowah*, in 2006 on Superphonic Records. The album was written during a thirty-day sentence that Johnston served in the Etowah County jail for drug possession.

"I was released into a men's home called Rapha [located in Attalla, Alabama]," Johnston said. "All I had ever been was a chef and a professional musician. They asked what I wanted to do, so I said that I wanted to write a book and a record. They created a job for me where I drove guys to their factory jobs at 8:00 a.m. After my job was done each day, I'd come back and write songs all day and pick them up in the afternoon."

A.A. Bondy. *Courtesy of Tell All Your Friends Publicity.*

During his time at Rapha, Johnston began using the name "Duquette" instead of Daniel. "I was a big fan of [singer-songwriter] Daniel Johnston," he said. "And I didn't want people to think that I was trying to use his name to create my own success. A press person tried to get me to once, and I told them that was bullshit."

Nuby founded Vulture Whale, another raw rock and roll band based in Birmingham. "When I moved home from Los Angeles, Jake Waitzman and Wes McDonald had started a band, and I thought, 'Oh, it might be fun to play guitar in that band,'" said Nuby of creating Vulture Whale. "And again, in the blink of an eye, it's been a decade."

Johnston continues his solo career, with his latest release produced by John Agnello (Sonic Youth, Dinosaur Jr., Kurt Vile). He also owns and operates a clothing and supply shop, Club Duquette, with his wife in Woodlawn.

Anne-Marie Griffin and Nick Daviston left music. The former earned a master's degree before getting married and moving to Utah. The latter is now the owner of Daviston Insulation in Birmingham.

In 2019, A.A. Bondy released *Enderness*, his first new studio album in eight years.

7

BIRMINGHAM'S DIRTY
LITTLE SECRET

I got a call from Twiggs Lyndon Jr.," Dan Nolen said of the event that set his course in stone. Lyndon had managed the Allman Brothers Band until the band parted ways and had booked shows at Nolen's Jacksonville, Alabama club Brothers Bar for Dixie Dregs. "'This weekend, you've got the Nighthawks,' he said to me. 'Look, nobody knows this, but Gregg Allman is divorcing Cher, and he's flying to Atlanta. I'm gonna bring him up, and he thinks I'm taking him to Macon to start doing drugs again, but I'm gonna bring him to Jacksonville, Alabama, this Saturday night to see the Nighthawks and get back into music. He's turned into a pop icon. He's on the cover of *People* magazine, and he's quit playing music. I've got to get him going again."

Brothers Bar opened in Jacksonville, Alabama, in 1976, shortly after Nolen graduated college and shortly after the State of Alabama overturned a law prohibiting bars from being located within one mile of a state university. The bar was an instant success, as artists had long sought a stop between Atlanta and New Orleans, and Birmingham had previously offered little reliability. There was the Wooden Nickel and Al's Crossroads, but there was still a large void in the market, and Nolen knew that he could fill it.

"I said, 'Twiggs, if I tell everybody in this small, little town that Gregg Allman is gonna walk through the door on Saturday night and jam with the Nighthawks, I'll never hear the end of it if it doesn't happen,'" said Nolen. "He said, 'I'm Twiggs Lyndon Jr. I'm giving you my word. I'll have Gregg there between 10:00 and 11:00 [p.m.]. You just have it packed.' So I said,

'Okay.' And I told everyone in town and I looked like a laughingstock. People were like, 'Gregg Allman is coming to Jacksonville on Saturday night? Yeah. That'll happen when pigs fly.'"

In 1977, Jacksonville's population was a little less than 10,000. It was a bit smaller than the estimated 600,000 who attended Summer Jam at Watkins Glen in 1973. Skepticism was easy.

"My old drinking buddies were all looking at their watches saying, 'What time is it man? What time is it?'" Nolen said. "And I was sweating bullets. And at about 10:45 [p.m.], Twiggs Lyndon Jr. walked Gregg Allman right through the front door. And that place erupted. I met him, we had a couple of beers and he met the band during their break and asked them, 'Is it okay if I get up and play a couple of tunes with you guys?' They said sure. That was one of the most memorable nights of my life. Gregg Allman was one of my musical heroes, and I had him in my bar. Gregg proceed to join the Nighthawks for about a year. So he came back into Jacksonville four or five times with the Nighthawks."

That's how "Birmingham's dirty little secret" began. Jacksonville may have been eighty miles northeast, but the Nick would have never become the place where Widespread Panic began its career in front of twelve people without Brothers Bar. The Nick never would have become the legendary club that hosted Red Hot Chili Peppers, Dave Matthews Band, Arcade Fire, the Black Crowes and Jane's Addiction or the club that Alice Cooper's band snuck into on a weeknight to play before his sold out show at the much larger Alabama Theater a few blocks away. It would have become the venue that Jason Isbell swung by after selling out the Alabama Theater just to hug some necks and pay respects.

After Gregg Allman made his appearance at Nolen's bar, Nolen began to seek out a new audience. Between Charlie Daniels, Allman's regular appearances in his club and Birmingham's void, Nolan knew that he could attract out-of-towners. He began advertising on Birmingham's 99.5 FM—all DIY.

"I got a call out of the blue from Tony Ruffino, who was the promoter in Birmingham," said Nolen. "He moved to Birmingham to stake out the Birmingham-Jefferson Civic Center. He'd do bigger shows like Earth, Wind and Fire, John Cougar Mellencamp, Fleetwood Mac. I had been looking for a place in Birmingham when he called me and asked, 'How are you getting all of these bands and who is writing all of your ads?' I said, 'I do. I write them.'"

Nolen drove to Birmingham and met with Ruffino, who admitted that he had also been seeking a smaller venue for shows in the Magic City. The two agreed to share ownership of the club they had both individually sought, which became Brothers Music Hall in Homewood. That room was a little large, holding one thousand people, making it difficult to fill on a Monday or Tuesday night. But it was the first time that Birmingham had been able to fill that niche.

Hank Williams Jr., the Police, the Ramones, Bob Marley, Elvis Costello, Dire Straits, Toto, Pat Benatar, Warren Zevon and John Prine all played Brothers Music Hall in the former Hollywood Country Club location on Shades Creek Parkway. In just two years, Nolen had gone from running a college bar in Jacksonville to a club that was hosting some of the biggest up-and-coming acts in the world.

"It was ironic, because I thought that we'd take the Wooden Nickel out within two or three months," Nolan said. But the Wooden Nickel maintained its audience, and Brothers Music Hall closed. There was a gas shortage and the nights, which happened more often than not, when the venue didn't have a premier act. It became too challenging to survive. Ruffino would later open Five Points Music Hall on Twentieth Street. This club had a very successful run of its own in the '90s.

"I took a few months off," Nolen said. "I went back to Brothers and worked to build that back up. There was a band called the Fitts that would pack out Brothers Thursday, Friday and Saturday. They asked me to manage their band. I told them they'd need to branch out, so I booked them into the Wooden Nickel, which was then owned by Bill Drennan. He didn't like the way his staff was running the place. The same weekend that I had the Fitts playing the club, he closed the venue and fired the staff. He gave me the keys, told me to put together a staff and run it, and he'd see me on Monday."

That was on a Thursday. They reconvened, and Nolen presented Drennan with an envelope that contained $500. Perplexed, Drennan asked what he was being given, and Nolen described it as his share of the weekend's profits.

"He said, 'Son, that's more money than I've made out of this place in two years,'" Nolen said. "He said, 'Here's the key. Give me $1,000 a month and it's yours.' I told him I'd have to make some changes, and he said, 'I don't care what you do, just get me $1,000 a month.' And I said, 'Done.' It was divine intervention. The club that I had set out to overtake was now my club."

He didn't have much money for the new spot. A painter came out and painted over "Wooden" and "el" on the sign outside of the venue, leaving "The Nick." That was June 22, 1982. After the City of Birmingham banned smoking in clubs in 2012, it became a little less hazy inside the wooden walls, but it still holds many of the same staples that pinned up signed band promotional photographs thirty years ago.

The Nick became the godfather of Birmingham clubs. It remains private, so it's notorious for hosting late shows, as no curfew is enforced. As Birmingham's scene grew and the market became more competitive, one constant remained: The Nick. Before Cave 9 was adding local acts to the bills of touring bands, and before BottleTree did the same, the Nick was there to give local artists an audience. From Telluride through Brother Cane and from Wayne (named by Pam Stallings) through Wray, Birmingham owes much to the Nick.

Pam Stallings frequented Brothers, and upon graduating college shortly after Nolen opened the Nick, she began working as a waitress. She moved to tending bar and quickly ascended to assistant manager and general manager before Nolen decided that he wanted a bigger challenge. He didn't want to compete with Ruffino's 5 Points Music Hall, so he left for Atlanta. He now owns Smith's Olde Bar in Atlanta.

That's when Stallings took over. She assured Nolen that she had no intentions of leaving Birmingham, as her family was in nearby Cullman. Nolen continues to book the Nick and has assured her that he always will.

Dexateens performing at the Nick. *Photo by Don Naman.*

"It's two places in one," Nolen said. "It's a great blue collar bar for folks that work day jobs and want to come have a few before they go home. Then you have soundcheck at 8:00 [p.m.], and that's when the noise starts, so those guys say, 'Okay, it's time to go.' They do soundcheck, we open the doors around 9:00 and have between three and five bands seven nights a week."

The Nick holds 250 people generously. It is in a section of Birmingham where St. Vincent's Hospital, the Highland Park community and the Southtown housing project meet. A rather perfect representation of Birmingham's spirit and grit, it seems nothing will ever kill it. While other rooms have come and gone, none have survived as the Nick has.

"The Nick wasn't the first thing I did in Birmingham, it was the second thing I did in Birmingham," said Nolen. "And that's why I've always been in favor of smaller rooms. You have a bigger room with five hundred people in it, and it still looks empty. You can put fifty people in the Nick, and it still looks packed. But you can still get a couple hundred more."

8

LEGACY

When Monroeville native Damon Johnson set out to form a rock and roll band, there was no real blueprint. Not in Birmingham, anyway. It was the early '90s—Muscle Shoals had a sound, Athens, Georgia, had a sound and Nashville had a different sound entirely. But in Birmingham, the closest thing to a blueprint was drawn by Hotel.

Incidentally, it was Hotel that gave Johnson his first big break. Split the Dark had formed out of the remnants of the '70s Magic City mainstays, and the group asked Johnson to join on guitar.

"I was twenty-two," Johnson recalled. "I was playing in a band from North Alabama that had just happened to play Louie Louie's in Southside, Birmingham on a no-cover Tuesday night. Marc Phillips, the lead singer of Hotel, who was then the lead singer of Split the Dark, just happened to come in that night and heard me play.

"They had been talking about adding another guitarist, and I was a fan. I used to see them play fraternity parties down at Auburn, and these guys were just out-of-their-mind talented. They didn't even ask me to audition—they just asked me to join their band! And I was like, 'Yes, I would!'

"And I can't put a proper measurement on—I wouldn't be talking to you right now if it weren't for that phone call. I'd never thought about moving to Birmingham. I was content being on Sand Mountain. I was playing in a band. We were making okay money on the weekends. I was thinking of transferring to a four-year school and getting an engineering degree. If it hadn't have been for that phone call from Marc, I might still be in Dekalb County right now."

Brother Cane began at the encouragement of Birmingham's Conrad Rafield, who was managing Split the Dark, Marc Phillips's post-Hotel project. He helped Johnson find a band, a place to rehearse and even housing for one of the band's first drummers. Brother Cane just needed a sound.

"At the time, there is no way I could have [given credit for Brother Cane's sound] with any real perspective," Johnson said. "I think our sound was shaped by the music that was happening right then. I say this without regret or without any shame: I wanted to be some version of the Black Crowes and Guns N' Roses. Those two records blew me away. I was disenfranchised with the '80s glam hair band thing. I didn't have anything to connect the dots with that. I didn't really go to college, so I didn't get exposed to the new wave thing or the college band thing. For me, it was the radio. I had grown up on the radio and the rock music that was starting to happen."

Johnson fancied himself the guitar player, and he needed a vocalist. But when the band was in danger of losing its development deal with Virgin Records because it couldn't find one, he stepped to the microphone and became the frontman.

"I didn't have influences as a singer," he said. "I had a ton of influences as a guitar player, but none as a singer."

When Brother Cane disbanded in 2000, Johnson found his greatest international successes. He had misses—Slave to the System, Red Halo and Whiskey Falls. And he had a brief stint in Damn Yankees, a cowriting credit on "Every Day" for Fleetwood Mac and backing guitar for the likes of Faith Hill. But in 2004, he joined Alice Cooper's band for five years. The bills became a little easier to pay.

He left Cooper in 2011 for Thin Lizzy. And somewhere along the way, he left the Magic City because being a working musician with a wife and children was easier to accomplish a few hours away in Nashville.

"There are a lot of people in my professional life that live here [in Nashville]," said Johnson. "And my wife and kids know a lot of those people. It was almost like built-in infrastructure for families with husbands that travel—sometimes for great lengths of time. It's important to me for my family to have that support when I'm out of town."

Thin Lizzy hadn't recorded new music as Thin Lizzy since founder, bassist and vocalist Phil Lynott died in 1986. The band continued to tour, in many forms, but 1983's *Thunder and Lightning* remains its final studio work. But its longest continuous members, guitarist Scott Gorham and keyboardist Darren Wharton, wanted to write new music. When Damon Johnson joined the band in 2011, its future become clearer.

"I was a little surprised when I joined to hear Scott Gorham say that he was seriously considering making a new Thin Lizzy album," Johnson said. "And there are a lot of ramifications to that—Phil Lynott was a legend, an icon and he passed away thirty years ago this past January. We all knew that it wouldn't be right to put out new music and call it Thin Lizzy without Phil in the band singing lead and playing bass guitar. So that's why we came up with a new name—Black Star Riders celebrates that legacy."

The band came to life, and Ireland embraced the new band name for its good intentions.

"It was important to [create a new band name] because we knew how passionate those fans were for that music," he said. "Thin Lizzy music isn't easily definable. You can't really put it in a category. It's classic rock, but there's nothing cheesy about Thin Lizzy's music. Phil Lynott was a poet. The songs had very musical arrangements, a lot of dynamics—a lot of people considered Thin Lizzy a musician's band.

"Ricky Warrick, who is the singer now, he and I grew up on Thin Lizzy, and we're as respectful and protective of that legacy as anyone. We knew that it was the right thing to do. It was not an easy transition. I've had so much experience in attempting to start new bands since Brother Cane officially hung it up in 2000, and as we get older—as people have personal lives and mortgages and commitments—it's just not as easy to jump in a van or bus for ten, twelve, fourteen or sixteen weeks as it was when we were in our late twenties."

The challenges of the new millennium's technology weren't easy to navigate. MTV and terrestrial radio didn't exist in the forms that Johnson and his peers had known. While he concedes that the internet was beneficial, getting new music in front of a new audience was the biggest challenge.

"The only way to do that is to tour," he said. "That first year was pretty tough. There were moments when I was scratching my head thinking, 'Wow. This is as hard as I thought it was going to be.' And the difference maker for us was the quality of the new songs. We've put out two albums now—pretty honest twin-guitar, harmony-based classic rock. Great lyrics and great performances. We're realistic that we're not going to become the Rolling Stones, but we love the music, we respect each other, and we enjoy playing together. That's why we continue to do it and why we'll continue to do it."

Johnson's story continues to add memorable chapters—some more memorable than others. "Every band that I've started, I've hoped that it could be its own productive entity," Johnson said. "By being productive, I hope that we can generate record sales and generate interest in seeing the band perform live and ultimately, that we can generate a living and continue getting to keep doing music as a full time endeavor. I couldn't get Slave to the System off the ground because everyone was in different bands. Whiskey Falls sure gave it a good shot—that band had so much potential, but our record company fell apart, so we didn't have the tour support, and we couldn't find another deal. My whole [life] is filled with stories of high hopes of multiple startups, but none of them ever reached critical mass."

The highest-profile gigs, Alice Cooper and Thin Lizzy, gave Johnson stability, but at fifty-two, he still aims for longevity under his own name. "Those are known entities, but in both cases, I was essentially a hired gun," he said. "I'm passionate about writing music and expressing myself creatively, and that's what I finally have in Black Star Riders. I have a great partner in Ricky Warrick, and we write the bulk of the material, but we also have a cool story with the Lizzy legacy. Somehow in the midst of a lack of interest in rock and roll, we're succeeding. As long as we continue that upward trajectory, there's no reason to bail out."

Echo is the solo effort that he released on March 18, 2015. He wrote and recorded the album in between Black Star Riders obligations, and it's been handled with care by Grammy award–winning rock producer Nick Raskulinecz (Foo Fighters, Alice in Chains, Deftones, Mastodon, the Hold

Damon Johnson. *Courtesy of Damon Johnson.*

Steady). Raskulinecz worked with Johnson on the second Black Star Riders record, and he offered his services again after their wives became friends.

"He came to me and said, 'If you have any solo material, you're welcome to come into the studio and use it,'" Johnson said. "And there was no way I was going to pass up an opportunity like that to work with him. I'm really grateful to Nick, and he has a huge part in how this sounds."

While Johnson doesn't deny the possibility of Brother Cane ever playing again, it's a long shot. Black Star Riders drives the bus now, but Johnson still hopes to one day take that control. *Echo* is the foundation of that dream.

"'Damon Johnson' is something that I want to continue to move toward," he said. "There's not a week that goes by that I don't get asked about Brother Cane, that I don't get asked about Alice Cooper or Whiskey Falls or Slave to the System or any of the other things that I've done. One of the greatest results of Black Star Riders is that it has really reignited my confidence in myself as a singer, as a writer—just the drive to put myself out there. I've certainly learned a lot about not only fronting a band, but leading a band since we were in Brother Cane, and this is finally my outlet to do that. And it's a bonus that I have this vast barrel of material now that I can draw from live."

9
ZYDECO

I n 1989, Steven Knight opened Zydeco in Southside Birmingham as a Cajun restaurant and venue for bluegrass and blues bands. Only the first floor existed then. The only Birmingham club that has stood longer is the Nick, which opened in 1984. As such, it's easy to romanticize the Nick's storied past while forgetting how vital Zydeco's contribution to the Magic City music scene has been. The list of young acts who have performed on Zydeco stage is equally impressive.

Alison Krauss and Union Station were there in 1993. Dave Matthews joined Tim Reynolds there in 1995. Counting Crows opened for Cracker at Zydeco in 1993. John Mayer, Train, Lemonheads, Shovels and Rope, Drive-By Truckers, Jason Isbell, Blues Traveler, Son Volt, Black Rebel Motorcycle Club, Medeski, Martin and Wood, Chris Stapleton, Snow Patrol and Justin Townes Earle, among many others, played Zydeco on their way up. And Zydeco saw Sum 41 on its way down. It saw Montgomery's Jamey Johnson join Lit for a version of the latter's "Miserable." And in 2016, Scott Weiland performed with his last band before his death, the Wildabouts. A then little-known, now Grammy-nominated band named Highly Suspect opened that show.

In 2003, Josh Billue bought the club, and shortly thereafter, Layne Flournoy began working for him. He tended bar, booked shows and managed. As Flournoy was then a recent UAB graduate with a degree in political science, the plan was law school, but as his presence within the club became more imposing, his course changed.

"Needless to say, that conversation with my parents—when I called to tell them, 'Hey, I'm going to manage this bar and not go to law school,'" Flournoy paused and laughed, "It's all good now, though."

Flournoy pressed harder, moonlighting as a talent buyer for other markets. Notably, he's promoted shows at Atlanta's Peachtree Tavern, Auburn's Bourbon Street and Tuscaloosa's Gallette's. Meanwhile, Billue had moved to Nashville after purchasing Exit/In, turning day-to-day operations of Zydeco to Flournoy.

"I started booking and promoting shows in other markets and saved where I could, and slowly, I was able to buy [Billue] out," Flournoy said. "He was very detached from the market. It just made sense for everybody." Billue had shown Flournoy the ropes, and while the two men are now separated by 190 miles, he remains a close friend and mentor.

Flournoy became the club's third owner just nine years after finishing his last class at UAB, and since then, diversity has been one of the club's two most important tenets. While Flournoy never fancied his venue better than any of the others in Birmingham, he aimed to make it Birmingham's most diverse. And it's difficult to argue with the results.

"In any given week, we'll have a metal show and a bluegrass show and a country show and a rap show and an indie rock show," Flournoy said. "It's tough to keep up with all of those genres of music, but because I also buy talent for college markets, I stay in tune with what college kids want. And if they want it, I want to sell it to them."

The genres that Zydeco has owned in Birmingham have been rap, country and EDM. Big K.R.I.T., Sam Hunt, Bassnectar, Run the Jewels, Dierks Bentley, Pretty Lights, Yelawolf, Luke Bryan, Flux Pavilion, Waka Flocka Flame and Little Big Town played Zydeco on the way up. Eric Church played there. Flournoy has booked Zac Brown Band shows for so long that he once negotiated a show with Brown for a percentage of the door (that show was at Auburn's Bourbon Street, but Brown has played Zydeco four times).

As Birmingham's music community has grown, Flournoy has made his second tenet to become a fabric of the UAB community that he grew to love as a student, inhaling sandwiches at Fat Sam's Sub Station on the Southside. He knows that a venue's sustainability depends on the crowd it could attract on the twenty days each month that it doesn't have a show.

"Sometimes it's not about how sexy your calendar is, it's about market demand," he said. "There was a time when no one was at Zydeco unless there was a big show upstairs. But now, I focus more on regular business. I

Shooter Jennings
performing at Zydeco.
Courtesy of Don Naman.

cater to the college kids. I went to UAB. I was very active when as a student. I take pride in UAB. When kids say, 'Hey, we're going to the bar tonight,' their friends don't say, 'Which bar?' They know which bar they're going to. And I like having that reputation."

Birmingham's second-oldest rock club, the "official Atlanta Braves bar of Birmingham," Southside's forgotten gem—over twenty-seven years, Zydeco has been a lot of things to a lot of people, but as the scene grows and the market becomes even more competitive, its most unique distinction has been its loyalty to the home team.

"I'm a part of the alumni society, and even when UAB wasn't doing very well in football, I bought season tickets every year," Flournoy said. "UAB was really good to me. I learned a lot outside of the classroom. There's no rhyme or reason to learning how to do what I do for a living. But I owe a lot to that school for the life experiences that I had while I was at that school. I love UAB."

10

MAYFIELD

M oses Mayfield's first independent release, *Enough to Let Go*, made the five-piece band a Birmingham household name in 2004. In 2007, Moses Mayfield signed a major record label deal. The band was opening for acts like Pete Yorn, the Fray, Switchfoot and Blue October. It was a tale not unlike other bands of the time—a young, talented, rising star was offered big promises that didn't quite pan out as hoped.

"The deals back then were absurd," said Matthew Mayfield. "It was almost like the housing crisis—they were giving out loans to bands that hadn't earned it yet. I had paid my dues—I had been playing in bands since I was thirteen or fourteen, playing anywhere I could get a gig, whether that was a birthday party or a fraternity party or the Nick. Wherever I could play."

The music business was changing—largely a reflection of the nation's economic struggles. Radio was being taken over by conglomerates, and the way that people consumed music was evolving. But when Mayfield's band inked the deal, the old model had yet to collapse.

"We got signed when I was twenty-one," said Mayfield. "The GM of Sony put his arm around me—we were playing with Pete Yorn, a sold-out show at Roseland Ballroom in New York City—and he puts his arm around me and says, 'You're going to be the next biggest rock band in the world, how does that feel?'

When you're twenty-one, and you hear those words, you believe them. I certainly don't buy them anymore. It's important—now that I've learned so much over the years—to respect the work that you have to put into it. The goal isn't to be a rock star, it's to be a career artist."

The economic downswing affected the label, and the young band from Birmingham joined many inside and outside the industry as a victim of the time.

"I have nothing but respect for Sony and Epic and Columbia—it was just politics," said Mayfield of the way the major relationship came. "Rick Rubin came in to run the label. He fired all the people, and naturally, like any corporation, when a new guy comes in and fires everybody, you're going to get fired, too. That ended up being the best thing that ever happened to me. I learned that this is a blue-collar industry, and you've got to work from the bottom up, not from the top down."

As the industry evolved, so did Mayfield. When he was a solo artist, he began releasing material digitally as he created it, no longer waiting on traditional full-length LPs. This new plan to be a career artist began as a challenge from his manager. "He had said, 'You're a prolific songwriter. You really seem to churn them out. Why don't we see if we can do an EP every month? Because why not?'" said Mayfield.

And so it was. From the time that Moses Mayfield dissolved in 2008 until 2010, Matthew Mayfield released *The Fire, Five Chances Remain Hers, Maybe Next Christmas, Breathe Out in Black, Man Made Machines* and *You're Not Home* as EPs. (He collaborated with Muscle Shoals native John Paul White of the Civil Wars on "Fire Escape," a track that was remixed with White's vocals on the 2013 EP *Irons in the Fire.*) With thirty-six new tracks on six releases in just more than two years, Mayfield had proven to himself that he was still a gifted writer. This led to his full-length solo debut, *Now You're Free,* in 2011.

"It became a challenge, but at the same time, it was an honor to put out that much music on your own dime and to see the response from the fans," said Mayfield. "These days, an album seems like a dime tour, but a lot of people still know the deep cuts. Loyalty from your fans is the biggest honor, and at the end of the day, I do it because I want to find those people that can relate. They know what you're talking about. It's like a therapy group."

During that stretch, his music began getting licensed for television. In 2009, the track "First in Line" appeared on ABC's *Grey's Anatomy*, and just one year later, his music returned to the show's soundtrack with "Better." Mayfield has since had his music soundtrack shows like *Hart of Dixie, Ringer* and *The Path.*

Mayfield was always a little detached from the rest of the scene. Unlike the punk and alternative scene of the '80s and '90s, there was never a clear line that attached Mayfield's work to other artists in the Magic City. He's been backed by many of Birmingham's most talented musicians, but since

Matthew Mayfield. *Courtesy of Sideways Inc.*

Moses Mayfield, those musicians have rotated a lot. His product is now clearly his own.

"I'm really proud of everyone that has been a part of the musical culture here," he said, "even people that are stylistically really different than me—I have a lot of respect for their artwork. I have a lot of respect for my friends from Birmingham that are doing really well and keeping us on the map. And I want to do the same thing. I want to make sure people know that we are representing a city and a culture and we're really proud of it. Nashville isn't the only place in the South for rock and roll and for music; there's so much talent here. There are bands doing two nights at the Alabama Theater, and that's amazing. There are national acts that come through that could never do that.

"It's evolved. Everyone realizes you have to work at it. You can't just be a superstar overnight. That happens occasionally—for the Justin Biebers of the world—but for the rest of us that believe in the art form, we've got to work our way up, continue to grind, continue to play every possible show we can and give the most passionate performance we can possibly give."

Mayfield's world was a bit dark before his 2016 release *Recoil*, which produced some of his most sincere and revealing work in a decade of proliferation. "Well, the lights went out," he said. "It was the hardest time of my life, personally, for about two months. The whole thing is set around grief, but grief doesn't have to be bad. There are songs like 'Indigo,' which are hopeful. You lose somebody you love; you see them on the other side. But then there are songs like 'God's Fault,' which is a fan favorite—it's brutal. It's a brutal song about betrayal."

He'd love to get the band back together one day, but he won't go it alone. "Everyone would have to be there," said Mayfield. "It would have to be all five of us. I wouldn't do it with a hired gun. We had a really special thing, and we spent a lot of long nights banging those songs out. Even though I was a young kid and I wrote all of the music, I'm still proud of that record. If they agreed to it and wanted to do it, I'd totally be in."

Mayfield released *Gun Shy* in March 2019.

11

THE X

WRAX-FM became one of the most important alternative radio stations in the country at the turn of the millennium. The Birmingham frequency broke Matchbox Twenty, Train and John Mayer, among others. The latter two each released official live records from Birmingham venues.

"Those guys would stay at my house," said Scott Register, local disc jockey and radio personality, of Train. "The whole band—two in one bedroom, four in the other. On a futon. Days at a time. And the first time Mayer came to town, he didn't have a guitar. Thankfully, we had a guitar, and he picked it up, and he made sounds that I didn't know a guitar could make. [Train and Mayer] are special to me because they sum up why I do what I do. In the case of Train, I wasn't working for Don [VanCleave, former owner of Magic Platter and first president of the Coalition of Independent Music Stores] yet, and I'd go to his office and sift through his promo box. There was one with a drawing of a kid with a crown on his head, and I asked him what it was."

He casually tossed the Train CD in his car, completely unaware that he was about to be the San Francisco band's first step in selling more than ten million albums worldwide.

"I reached back for it one day, and I heard 'Meet Virginia,' and I knew that was a hit song," Register said. "And it just happened that they were coming to Birmingham for Zydeco Fest. So, they came by my show that

Sunday, and something went wrong with my board. Dave [Rossi] came in to run the board. They played [Led Zeppelin's] 'Ramble On,' and Dave lost it. The label wasn't sure that they believed in them until they were sent a video of everyone at X Fest singing along to 'I Am' and 'Meet Virginia.'"

That was the power of Scott Register and 107.7 The X in 1998. It became as integral to Birmingham's musical identity as anything that had come before—Tuxedo Junction, Hotel and Telluride, the punk rock and DIY scene that grew from the '80s, St. Paul and the Broken Bones. The radio station brought emerging artists to town and put them on small stages, and Birmingham's venues remained the foundation of its "scene."

"I got a call from a listener that had gone to a show at Eddie's Attic [in Decatur, Georgia]," said Register. "[John Mayer] had opened. Don started selling sixty CDs a week, and he was keeping John alive in Atlanta."

Building a Bear

The X behemoth began with 105.9 The Bear, an active rock station with a Class A three-thousand-watt radio station with a tower in Trussville, Alabama. In 1996, Davis Hawkins, then with Dick Broadcasting, leased the station from its owner, fired the existing staff and hired Luka (morning drive), Rossi (middays) and "Hurricane" Shane (afternoon drive), the original staff at The X. Rossi had recently lost his job at 96 Wave in Charleston after several management changes, but he'd developed quite a reputation among record labels and industry executives for his ear for music. That's when Hawkins lured his program director to the Magic City.

Hawkins then purchased WENN, an urban station at the 107.7 dial position that was struggling to compete with 95.7 Jamz and KISS-FM 98.7. He flipped 107.7 with 105.9 in 1998. Luka departed (for the first time), and the morning team of Beaner and Ken made its debut.

"Jamz and KISS were already kicking butt," Hawkins said. "So WENN was pretty much dead. The Seattle grunge scene had been kicking hard—Pearl Jam, Chili Peppers. All the singer-songwriters were coming along—Dave Matthews, Blues Traveler, Alanis Morissette, Sheryl Crow, Cowboy Mouth, Live. All these bands that never existed started coming along, and I thought, 'Man, there's a whole new wave of music coming, and it's alternative.' That's when I decided to make that flip."

The station was modeled on 99X in Atlanta. When Hawkins made the decision to flip the two stations, he let Rossi steer the ship.

"Dave came from a Charleston radio station called 96 Wave," Hawkins said. "There were basically three radio stations in the Southeast that controlled the music: 96 Wave in Charleston, 99X and 107.7. If you could get radio airplay on those three stations, you were gonna be a rock star. The record labels camped out there. Me and Rossi would have lunch, and we'd come back, and Train is sitting in the lobby. Matchbox Twenty is in the lobby. Dave Matthews is in the lobby. Bush is in the lobby. They're all just sitting up there saying, 'Please, please, please play our record.' Birmingham had that much power over music back in the '90s."

Hawkins recalls paying artists like Maroon 5 and Dave Matthews Band $500 to play 5 Points Music Hall. Many artists, he says, played Birmingham for free.

"Most of them came through Birmingham and just wanted me to play their records," he said. "Because if I played their records, Atlanta was watching everything I was doing, and Charleston was watching everything I was doing. But I was watching Atlanta and Charleston. These three radio stations were the heartbeat of alternative—they controlled it all in the Southeast."

Register joined the staff in January 1997. He had been working at McCullough Advertising, the firm that did public relations and marketing for City Stages, the defunct festival that relied on The X to lure its talent. It was at City Stages that Register and Rossi first shared their musical tastes and their love for breaking new music. Rossi offered Register, who had never been on radio, a one-hour Sunday morning program, which would become Reg's Coffee House. Reg's input shaped the station as much as Rossi's—both men had impeccable taste.

"Reg was the first guy in America to play Train," said Hawkins. "He was the first guy in America to play Matchbox Twenty. I believe he was the first guy to play Fastball. There are a lot of bands that Reg was the first one to give airplay. We tested music on Reg's show. His show was so alternative. If music did well on his show, we'd put it in regular programming. Reg was really the foundation of testing a lot of new music. I didn't have to answer to iHeartRadio. I didn't have to answer to anybody. Me and Rossi would play whatever the hell we wanted to play. Now you can't do that."

"Since I was a little kid, I just loved good songs," Register said. "Thank God my ears work. That's about all that works right. There's no science or empirical formula. I hear a song and get a gut feeling that people want to hear it. Music has been a part of me for as long as I can remember. That's how my mom and I connected from my earliest memories, listening to a

The X staff, circa 1990s.
Photo by Geno Pearson.

record, buying a record, going to concerts from when I was as young as five or six years old."

That kid from McCullough Advertising wasn't paid for his hour slot. He didn't want to be. "I wouldn't let him," Register said. "I wanted to do this. I didn't want anybody having any sway over what I was playing. I refused payment for a good eight years before Davis said, 'We have to pay you, or you can't do it anymore.'"

THE X BRAND

Live in the X Lounge became one of the most successful projects The X created. Each November, the station would release a compilation disc featuring performances that it had recorded with artists who were passing through town. The discs were sold exclusively at Blockbuster Video in the metropolitan Birmingham area, and all proceeds were donated to United Cerebral Palsy (UPC) of Greater Birmingham.

"We stole that idea from Atlanta," Hawkins said. "It was really easy to do. The bands were all agreeable because I gave all the money to UCP. We started off issuing five thousand copies, but they would sell out in four or five hours. After the first couple of *X Lounges*, I said, 'Damn, we need to increase this to ten thousand,' but the music kept coming. That was the key thing. The music just kept coming. Every time we would turn around, there was another fabulous alternative band coming out."

There was also X-Fest at Oak Mountain Amphitheater—the first of which was headlined by Matchbox Twenty. The inaugural show sold out of ten thousand tickets, and Hawkins says that the band played for free.

"I think Davis thought I was from Mars for the first five years I was there," said Register. "He'd just shake his head. But he didn't shake his head anymore when he went and saw a sold out amphitheater with people singing every word to songs that they first heard on my show."

"Those are the kinds of things that put a radio station over the top," Hawkins said. "When you're putting out CDs and you're out there doing concerts once a year, it makes your station bigger than life. The station was on the streets all the time. We created Beer, Bands and Bingo, which was one of the biggest radio promotions in the history of Birmingham. It was really a special time for radio. I was told by my consultants that it would never work, and I thought, 'You know what? I think it'll work.'"

THE EX

Dick Broadcasting sold its cluster of radio stations to Citadel Broadcasting in 2001. "That's when I essentially retired," said Hawkins. "I felt like I couldn't work for a publicly owned company because I felt like I created all of those radio stations. And now I've got Citadel coming in here and telling me what I need to do to run these radio stations? No. I'm not gonna do this. I built them, and when I took over all of those radio stations, they were basically in bankruptcy. I built them up. So I decided I was gonna go play golf."

"Radio killed the rock star," Hawkins said. "And it all happened around 2000—'99 through '01. Clear Channel was the catalyst of it all. They pretty much killed radio. The evolution of music consumption hasn't helped. People can build radio stations in their car on their iPod or on Pandora. But I still believe that if someone took over four or five radio stations and put DJs on—morning, midday, afternoon and night—and they answered the phone at night, took requests, talked about what's going on in Birmingham locally, what's going on with the weather, what's the concert at Oak Mountain Amphitheater tonight, what's going on at Iron City tonight, doors open at seven—if they would go back to local, local, local, local, I think radio would be great again."

"He would take chances," Register said of Hawkins. "But mainly, he would let people do their jobs and not micromanage."

When The X moved to a much weaker signal at 100.5 in 2006, the constant was Reg. He encouraged management to bring Rossi back. After Live 100.5 dissolved two years later and was born again as the internet-only Birmingham Mountain Radio in 2010, the centerpiece was Reg. Rossi was long gone to Nashville, but Reg had become such a fabric of the Birmingham scene that the new grassroots station wanted to be built around him.

Hawkins, who had a controlling interest in Summit Media, helped bring Birmingham Mountain Radio to terrestrial radio in 2013. The station had been broadcasting exclusively on the internet since 2010, when Geno Pearson, Jeff Clanton and Jeremy Harper decided to fill the void left by the death of Live 100.5, a concept devised over drinks at the Barking Kudu.

"As an internet station, we were already making strides against FM," said Birmingham Mountain Radio program director Geno Pearson. "The people at Summit Broadcasting took notice and wanted to be involved in the success of Birmingham Mountain Radio, so we became a partner with them when it came to ad sales."

That successful model was a combination of the old way—local hosts, local shows, local weather, local music mixed in—and a new way that involved shorter commercial breaks that leaned on ten-to-fifteen-second advertisements.

"They told us they wanted us to remain in control," Pearson said of the terrestrial radio station that finally lured the station away from the internet. "An 'If it ain't broke' kind of thing—they didn't think they could do it better. Unlike another company in town that approached Jeff and I and said, 'Time to stop this as a hobby and let us take it over.' That didn't fly at all."

The new station is a reimagined brand rooted in what Register, Rossi and Hawkins envisioned two decades before. "There are a lot of people that don't have the time to sift through new music," Register said. "As long as there are cars, and radio comes on in them for free, it will still succeed."

12

SEARCHING FOR A HIT

Damon Johnson and Brother Cane carried Birmingham's mainstream through hair metal and grunge into '90s alternative. The wave of bands that followed were led by acts like Suburban Love Junkies and Wayne and grew to include Adelayda, Mars Electric and Virgos Merlot. It was a mainstream scene that didn't begin with much help, but it was boosted by the arrival of 107.7 The X, a station that earned national fame for being the first in town to feature late 1990s and early 2000s alternative acts like Matchbox Twenty, Train and John Mayer.

SHOOTING AT THE STARS

Around 1991, Chalkville native Rodney Reaves started writing songs seriously. He was in his late twenties and was married. He'd been in bands before but nothing with real direction.

He already knew Jason Elgin, who would eventually produce Wayne's *Music on Plastic*, and they had begun writing some songs together. They'd played acoustically for a while until Elgin decided to open his own studio. Reaves helped build Elgin's studio, which was located above a clothing store in Tarrant, and at some point, everyone in the band lived there more or less. That studio was Synchromesh, and it became the home base for much of the scene. Virgos Merlot recorded there after signing with Jeff Hanson Management. (Hanson earned his reputation as the manager who discovered Creed.)

Michael Swann had been playing guitar with Jacob Bunton in Mars Electric and its predecessor, Wish, but Reaves recruited him after Elgin's departure. "I had set my sights on Michael and was just waiting until I had enough good stuff to convince him to come to the good side," Reaves joked.

Elgin later introduced Reaves to Jon Hornsby, who joined on drums.

"I knew Pam [Stallings] down at the Nick, so she kind of hooked us up with our first show," Reaves said. "She booked us. We'd hang out with everyone there—it was a huge family. So, when I told Pam we were finally ready to play live, she said, 'Absolutely. Let's do it.' So, she gave me a date. We're thinking on how we're gonna get people to come out, and she calls me a week later. 'So, what is the name of your band?' And I said, 'Actually, I haven't even thought about that.'"

That's when Stallings named the band. It was around 1994, and the band was a three-piece. Reaves recalls, "She said, 'Well, I need something to put on the marquee.' I said, 'Can I get back to you?' and she said, 'Well, I kind of need to do it now. What's your middle name?' And I said, 'Wayne.' So, she said, 'I'm gonna book it as Wayne, and you can deal with it later.' And I never dealt with it later. So, we were always Wayne."

Reaves found an investor, and Wayne cut the first version of its demo as 1995 turned into 1996. This was a project already nearly five years in the making.

"We printed it ourselves and sold copies," Reaves said. "Scott Register and Don VanCleave got interested in it, and we talked to them a lot. Brett [Hestla, of Virgos Merlot] had played on one song that we had done, and we were good friends with their band. He liked our band, he liked the stuff we were recording. So, I gave him the demo when we finished.

"He said, 'This is fantastic, I'm gonna give it to Jeff [Hanson].' He gave it to Jeff Hanson, their management, and it wasn't long before Jeff called and said, 'I love this stuff, I want to sign you guys to the management company.' It was exciting. We asked him some questions. We talked to the Virgos guys. They said, 'He's great. He manages Creed. He knows what he's doing.' So, we signed with Hanson."

Hanson immediately took Reaves to EMI Publishing in New York City with hopes of securing a publishing deal. After Reaves played five or six songs to a boardroom, the trip was a success. Rick Krim signed Reaves to a publishing deal with EMI.

"He said, 'Here's what we want to do: We want to sign you to a publishing deal, but we don't want to get you on a label just yet. We want to pay for you to go back, finish this record just like you guys did it with no interference, no opinions from anyone else telling you what to do. Because what you guys have done is great. Go back and finish it, and once the record is completely done—you feel like it's finished and we feel like it's finished—then we'll shop it to labels," Reaves said.

"And that was a big plus to me. I never wanted anyone to tell us how to do it. Because we were cocky back then. We thought we knew what we were doing. But we kinda did. We knew how we wanted everything to sound. We worked long hours. That's all we fricking did back then."

The band finished the record on its own. As promised, Krim kept his hands off, with one exception. Cover versions were hot, and he encouraged the band to choose one.

"I told him that I didn't play covers out live," Reaves said. "I'm not [just] a musician; I'm a songwriter. But then one day, for whatever reason, I had that '[Goodbye] Yellow Brick Road' song in my head, and I called Jason, and I said, 'What do you think about actually doing a cover song?' He said, 'Seriously? What song?' And I said, 'Yellow Brick Road,' and he said, 'Yeah, that'll work.'

"So, I called Rick, and I told him, and he said, 'No shit, which one?'" Reaves continued. "I told him, and he said, 'How much money do you need?'"

That cover was included on what was the third version of *Music on Plastic*, released on TVT Records around the turn of the millennium. It was also around that time that the first bassist parted ways and Keith and Kevin Harrison, formerly of Volant, joined the Wayne lineup.

The group picked up some shows with Better Than Ezra—a show at Five Points Music Hall, one in Nashville and another in Montevallo. It played City Stages and Music Maynia in Huntsville. It joined a Bob Schneider tour for an extended period and then another with John Mayer. The final major tour—and the biggest—was with the Tragically Hip. That's when Wayne began to wane.

"Part of the deal with EMI was that we had to sign with a major label," Reaves said. "[TVT Records] just met the requirements of being a major label. They had their own distribution. They wanted us with someone that could actually put something behind us. They were gonna do everything they could to make this band work, and that started out great.

"We put the first single out, we did radio interviews. But after the first single, things started feeling…not right. [Label founder Steve Gottlieb] had planned a video to be filmed, and he fired everyone on that before it was even finished. Things went downhill," Reaves continued. "He tried to talk me into going solo, which I never would have done. They put out the first single, which was hit and miss. The plan was that the next single goes out on this day, and the next tour starts here, but they just kind of started backing off on things. We're out with the Tragically Hip, which was a blast, but we were working our tails off."

TVT Records never put out the second single. Wayne was invited to go to Europe with the Tragically Hip, but TVT discouraged the band from making the trip. "So, I told them, 'I'm gonna go home,' Reaves joked. "And I went home and sat on my ass with the intentions of just letting that contract run its course and be done. Over the years, I just stopped playing. I came home. I had a daughter. A second one came a couple of years later."

That was around 2003. For all intents and purposes, that was the end of Wayne. Reaves continued working with Elgin at Synchromesh with other bands on occasion. He'd rewrite some lyrics and provide melody parts. But after a few years, he left the business. He left for a family and stability. He now lives near Trussville, Alabama.

WEIGHTLESS

Eric Watters first saw stages in Birmingham with his high school cover band that he formed with Matt Alexander. Eric's mom would check him out of school, and they'd play gigs at fraternity parties and proms on the weekend. He was a junior at Homewood High School when he first performed in front of audiences.

He enrolled at the University of Montevallo hoping to earn a degree in music. He quickly learned that wasn't for him and switched his major to English. It was around that time that he began Suburban Love Junkies with Jimmy Finney.

In 1995, the pair went to Airwaves Recording Studio in downtown Homewood and laid down the tracks that would become their debut. James played drums and guitar, and Watters played bass and guitar. They both sang.

Suburban Love Junkies got a production deal in Atlanta with Grammy-winning producer Don McCollister. That session produced *Weightless,* a double LP. The recording scored a deal with the New York–based Childlike Records. The band was on the road and playing about 250 shows a year.

"It was a good scene," Watters said. "There's not a scene anymore, I don't think. Back then, there was a definite thing going on—something was happening. Wayne got signed to TVT Records. Virgos Merlot got signed to a pretty big label. Blue Epic got signed. I had recorded all of their demo

Suburban Love Junkies. *Photo by* Eric Watters.

stuff before they got a deal. I thought that was the best period of music in Birmingham's history."

By 2004, Watters and Finney were touring exclusively as Caddle, a harder rock project. Caddle played shows with hard rock and southern rock artists from Lynyrd Skynyrd to Kid Rock to Cross Canadian Ragweed. Suburban Love Junkies never disbanded, but its touring slowed significantly as the new project became the focus. In 2018, Suburban Love Junkies finished its most recent record. The band has included Brant Benefield on drums and Josh Moehr on bass since approximately 2000.

Watters now lives in Leeds, Alabama, where he owns his own studio and does production work for artists from around the Southeast. At his studio, he's relied on the other guys in Suburban Love Junkies to play studio parts for several vocalists. He plays local shows with Suburban Love Junkies and Caddle a few times a year.

SOMEDAY

Jacob Bunton grew up in Tarrant, just down the road from Elgin's studio. He'd played in a punk band called Jade's Dream in the early '90s before recruiting Jesse Suttle from the Shame Idols and forming Wish in 1995. That formation was a bit accidental. Birmingham's Little Red Rocket had a show at the Rockin' Horse and needed an opener. Neither Jade's Dream nor the Shame Idols could fill the slot, and at Jesse's suggestion, the two formed what was originally a side project to play the set.

"I wrote eight songs in two days. We rehearsed twice and played the show," said Bunton. "A week later, we recorded the eight songs. We did the drums at Synchromesh Studios in Tarrant with Jason Elgin, and we did the rest with Ben Trexel."

Wish became Mars Electric in 1998. Bunton had gotten wind of other bands named Wish and needed a name change, so he went with Mars Electric—the namesake being a company in Tarrant that made electrical parts, owned by Gwen Mars.

"[Gwen] used to babysit a guy named Michael Thrasher, who moved to L.A. and started a band named Gwen Mars that was signed to Hollywood Records," Bunton said. "Gwen had two Birmingham bands with major label deals named after her."

Bunton's first deal was with Atlantic and then with Columbia. Suttle left before the deal was in place to focus his energy on the Shame Idols. Mars Electric and the Shame Idols were two very different sounds. Bunton's new direction was much more radio friendly—more mainstream. Mars Electric also earned rotation on 107.7 The X and was playing the same festival circuits as Wayne. And the Shame Idols was a punk band. Bunton perpetuated two very different versions of a Birmingham sound that have remained for nearly forty years. This was the conundrum of the Birmingham music scene—a scene reliant on its venues and club owners and that, despite overlap, never fully realized that its inspiration came from within itself.

"I don't think Birmingham ever had a 'sound,'" Bunton said. "All the bands in Birmingham were very diverse. We had the music scene because of the Nick, Zydeco, Louie Louie's, the High Note, 5 Points Music Hall, etcetera, but it wasn't the same as other places. We all just kind of did our own thing. Promoters would book the shows and throw the bands on, but everyone wasn't necessarily friendly or even friends."

Today, Bunton's accomplishments are numerous. He won an Emmy for television songwriting, toured as part of Steven Adler's band and has credits on work with Mariah Carey, Jennifer Lopez, Smokey Robinson and Akon. But without the generosity of Elgin and Trexel, Bunton insists he never would have seen that path.

"I grew up extremely dirt poor, and if it weren't for those two recording me for free, that eight-song record, which eventually led to a huge record deal, would have never happened," said Bunton.

Bunton continues his writing career in Los Angeles.

BREAKING

Unstrung played a lot of bills with Bunton and Swann's Wish. That was the group's first show, in fact, at the Rockin' Horse at the Colonnade. Unstrung was made up of Jackson Eppley on bass, Chris Griffin on guitar, Brian Todd on guitar, Scotty Chapman on drums and Jeff Holmes on lead vocals. The group put together a demo with Trexel and went to Synchromesh to record with Elgin. The album was never released.

Holmes was a little older than his bandmates, and when he moved to Jacksonville for school, he began playing solo. He'd already been playing at Brothers Bar and the Nick with Unstrung, so finding gigs wasn't difficult. In early 1998, he returned to Birmingham after a semester and played a song that he had been working on for Trexel called "Crowded Room." Trexel loved it.

Holmes and Trexel recorded all of the parts and released "Crowded Room" on a local compilation disc called *The Foundry*. The buzz from the release earned Holmes a spot on a bill at 5 Points Music Hall for a Christmas show with local acts. There, he met Suburban Love Junkies, which led to his recording with Eric Watters.

At the encouragement of his friends in Suburban Love Junkies, he worked solo on the earliest recordings of what would become Adelayda, a full band. This included "Separate Lives," "Crowded Room" and "Jersey." At least one third of what would become the debut album was his solo work. He wasn't very confident on stage, and the idea of being able to hide behind a band gave him some hope.

The original Adelayda lineup debuted in 2000. It began as a three-piece: Holmes, drummer Dan Baker and bassist Dave Mattson. They eventually added Eric Wingard as their first lead guitarist, shuffling through about seven more before settling on Justin Gannon. That was just before the group opened for Course of Nature, a band from Enterprise, Alabama, that had started getting national radio play with its single "Caught in the Sun."

"When we walked off stage, a pretty large portion of the crowd left," Holmes said. "It pissed off their manager because there wasn't a huge crowd in there to begin with. He went in the back to sulk, and his wife came up to him and asked, 'Did you see the opening band?' He hadn't, and she convinced him to listen to our demo. She had grabbed our demo that night, the stuff that we had recorded at Eric's."

Adelayda signed with Ronnie Gilley's Superkala Records in 2002—a management deal with a record option. They trekked to Ardent Studios

Adelayda. *Photo by Jeff Holmes.*

in Memphis to record three tracks. That EP included the recording of "Separate Lives," which quickly jumped into heavy rotation at 107.7 The X. It was picked up in Mobile, Alabama; Jackson, Mississippi; the Carolinas; and the Florida Panhandle. It was a regional smash in a time just before radio's homogeny—when markets chose their own favorites and local record shops tried to keep up.

Course of Nature had signed the largest deal that Atlantic/Lava had ever given to an unsigned band, and Gilley was convinced that he could maintain that momentum with Adelayda. The band moved to Chancellor, Alabama, just outside of Enterprise, to live and work together and create music. Eppley rejoined on bass at this time after completing a degree in music at Berklee College of Music.

The recording process was going smoothly, and Grammy-winner David Campbell had joined in the studio on strings.

"The problem that we faced is that when your manager is also your label, no one is really looking out for you," said Holmes. "And we weren't well-versed enough to understand when people were taking advantage of us."

The album was completed with a tentative release set for April 2003. It was delayed until October 2003. Superkala and Ronnie Gilley Entertainment weren't equipped for the distribution, and getting the record into stores proved virtually impossible.

"We would go play in FYE in Omaha, Nebraska," Holmes said. "Our song was number one on KCTY in Omaha, Nebraska. We're opening up for Sister Hazel that night. We're walking into the store and we were literally bringing the CDs into the store to sell because they didn't have a copy.

"The X started playing the old version of 'Not Tonight' because people wanted new music, so we immediately got the new version to them," Holmes said. "'Not Tonight' took off like a firecracker. It broke the regional success, and we started charting nationally—on Indicator more than Billboard, because Billboard isn't just radio play, it's sales, and we didn't have a record out. Every time I saw the pop contemporary charts then, it was us and Nelly, and that made me laugh"

"Not Tonight" became the most requested song in two dozen markets, according to Holmes. But the only places that people were able to acquire the song and record was via illegal download on Napster and Kazaa.

The six-month distribution delay killed the band's momentum. The label and the band both grew frustrated with distribution and sales. With a family at home, it was no longer financially responsible for Gannon to continue. Eppley moved to Los Angeles to play with Course of Nature. Then Holmes and Baker mutually parted ways.

Holmes moved to Atlanta for a girl and a fresh start and put together what he now affectionately calls "Adelayda 2.0," with Kevin Vines on bass, Jeff Gardner (who had been the lead singer of Georgia-based Union Drag) on guitar. Holmes rotated a few drummers and percussionists for shows throughout the summer of 2004. The label continued to struggle financially and eventually pulled all funding.

"With the original band having split up and all of my best friends in different places, as solid as those guys were, it just never felt like Adelayda again," Holmes said, "but we had obligations. We had people that had paid to see us. We had shows that were sold out. The album had just been released in October and now it was February. So we kept it going as long as we could."

Gilley had gotten heavily involved in country music and eventually organized the BamaJam festival near Enterprise. He took Holmes to Nashville that winter to audition for James Stroud at Dreamworks. He played a number of Adelayda songs with a country twist. Stroud and Holmes both knew that it wasn't a fit, and the idea quickly dissolved. The final Adelayda show was in September 2004.

SPACES AND FACES OF BIRMINGHAM'S SCENE

Ronnie Gilley spent four years in federal prison for his role in a bribery scandal that involved attempting to buy pro-gambling legislation for the state of Alabama. He was released in February 2017.

Holmes took on a full-time day job in Atlanta, eventually becoming chief operating officer. He has a daughter and still dabbles in music. He officially released his solo debut, an EP titled *The Shame and the Grace*, in May 2017.

13

COMMUNICATING VESSELS

Maybe Birmingham's music scene learned a lesson from its food scene. "Frank Stitt is somebody that I deeply respect," said independent record label Communicating Vessels founder Jeffrey Cain. "He left—had to go learn. And when he came back—all of the restaurants out there now—those guys worked under Frank. He's supported them. He's never looked at them as competition. He's instilled in them that cooking was a living art, not a dead one. If you strangle something and keep it for yourself—it's dead at that stage. If you pass it on, it's alive. And that's what's happening in the music scene now."

In the '90s and through the turn of the millennium, Birmingham music had a sharing problem. Maybe that was because of distrust, or maybe it was simply the fear that another band would get the gig. Breaking down that wall was Cain's aim.

The Mobile native and Remy Zero guitarist moved to the Magic City in 2008. A new Remy Zero project remained a possibility in Birmingham, the band's new home, but not in Los Angeles. Bassist Cedric Lemoyne and drummer Gregory Slay had also relocated. But when Slay passed away in 2010, Cain knew that he didn't want to be onstage again for a long time.

Communicating Vessels was born in 2011—a time long before vinyl had returned to mainstream masses. It began with a series of 7-inch singles in Cain's home studio. He wanted to establish the brand—to show that rock and experimental and hip-hop music could all exist under one Birmingham roof. With the packaging, he wanted to show that music could coexist with art. It became the first full-length eponymous release from Great Book of John, a band that rose from the ashes of Wild Sweet Orange.

"[Former Wild Sweet Orange guitarist] Taylor Shaw played me thirty songs that he had not released," Cain said. "That became Great Book of

John. When I made that, I was so in love with the band and the record that I knew that I didn't want to shop it. I didn't want to convince someone else that they had to like it. I wanted to put it out the way it needed to be put out. If there was going to be a first record on a label, I knew that would be one that I would be proud to have as the first record on my label."

As his roster added other Birmingham acts like the Green Seed, Wray, Shaheed and DJ Supreme and Future Elevators, Cain's vision became a showcase for a modern South left of the dial. As it turned out, Cain had no interest in the southern indie status quo.

"The traditional South has been fairly represented for a long time," he said. "Whether it's Americana or folk or country or blues or soul—all of those things are in our DNA. You grow up in it and around it. You grow up in churches playing music. You grow up with your uncles and aunts playing guitar better than what you are hearing on the radio. That's represented as it should be. When I was a kid putting out music, the bands that I was attracted to from the South were telling the South's story through a different lens."

That group of southern storytellers included the likes of Saturn owner Brian Teasley, Man or Astro-Man?, R.E.M. and the B-52s.

"I like showing the world things from this area that they wouldn't expect," Cain said. "When you hear this shoegaze, reverb-drenched band [Wray], you don't think that can come from the South. But when you get under that, I hear an amazing southern guitar player. He's playing through effects and a haze, but I hear southernness in those things. I hear it in the hip-hop. You could hear it in Verbena. You could even hear it in Remy Zero—in the voices, in the guitars. People didn't think we sounded like southern rock bands, but it's all there."

Just a couple of years ago, Cain traveled to the United Kingdom for Wray's first run of shows there. The BBC has played many of his artists, like Future Elevators. Shaheed and DJ Supreme cut tracks with hip-hop legends Jurassic 5 and Slug from Atmosphere.

Communicating Vessels was born of Cain's space in Woodlawn—a space that encouraged collaborative creativity in a part of Birmingham that was virtually abandoned.

"Even eight years ago, people weren't using and enjoying their city like they are now," he said. "The food scene got people out of their homes trying new restaurants. That led to people going to venues and checking out music. And with good radio and good local artists making original records, people began going to see things that weren't cover bands. People are enjoying the streets of this city. The more people do that, the more people join them and venture into areas of town that they haven't been, and I see people that are thankful to be in the city."

14

CAVE 9

There were rooms before Cave 9. There were four walls, a ticket taker at the door and somebody who wouldn't get paid to mop the sticky floor. There were rooms like the Tuxedo Junction Ballroom, which earned its name from neighboring Tuxedo Park in Ensley and became famous because of a tune that Erskine Hawkins played, right there where Birmingham's music history began. Long after the final jazz improvisation at the Tuxedo Junction Ballroom, it was just a room—a room where punk rock shows happened in Birmingham. Propagandhi played there once.

There were clubs and record shops before Cave 9 too—places like Big Dan's Fantastic Planet, American Beat Records and Unity. And, of course, there was always the Nick and Zydeco, the Rasputin and Magellan of do-it-yourself Birmingham. Cave 9 had about a seven-year run, after all. BottleTree followed and evolved into Birmingham's most ambitious do-it-yourself room, Saturn. The Forge followed and then Firehouse. Ten years from now and twenty years from then, new venues will come and go and someone else and some other scene will experience its own moment in time.

But on March 8, 2003, Aaron Hamilton opened Cave 9 at 2237 Magnolia Avenue in Birmingham's Southside with help from Angelica Hankins. Birmingham punk rock kids born between 1980 and 1990 greeted their own moment in time. It shared space with Alabama Art Supply at that time. The first bill featured Birmingham's Blue Eyed Boy Mr. Death, Haunted Stepdaughters, Death or El Dona, This Day Will Burn and High Speed Comic Collector from Anniston. The show was five dollars.

Those kids found their way to Hamilton and Hankins the same way the generation before them had found the house shows, keggers in church basements and Bubba Town.

"I came in on the first night and told Aaron and Angelica that I knew how to run sound and how to book shows," said Trent Thomas, who found the Birmingham scene in the late '90s, when he began playing and booking shows at Barnstormer's in Montevallo. Thomas was also part of Blue Eyed Boy Mr. Death. "I made myself available to them anytime they needed help."

By 2004, Thomas was taking on a more serious role as an associate director. He ran sound, helped bands load in and out of the venue and booked and promoted shows. He eventually served on the board of directors of Cave 9. As the Cave 9 crew expanded, every promoter and staff member that had a fingerprint on the venue agreed on one truism: all shows were all ages.

"I would rather not book a show than do a twenty-one-and-up show," said longtime promoter Mike Parsons. That's how kids—kids with nothing better to do, who felt alienated in their suburban schools, who needed to release some aggression, who weren't afraid to go downtown when their parents discouraged it—found Cave 9.

And Birmingham kids may have taken the whole thing for granted. For those who grew up in rural parts of Alabama, rooms like Cave 9 were even more special.

"Moving to Birmingham was a sort of revelation, which probably sounds strange whenever I say it to natives who generally revere the city much less than its transplants," said Will Butler, who spent several years working on and booking shows at the venue. Butler also served on the board of directors when Cave 9 became a nonprofit. "Even before Cave 9, the options for seeing live music were so much higher. I moved to town at the tail end of the Boiler Room era. I saw a few shows there, made the trip down to Montevallo for some shows at Barnstormers."

"I might be biased because I was at the perfect age," said Lee Bains III. "But for me, it was peculiar in its ability to build a sense of community and be a port in a storm. Most DYI venues before it and since have been marked by instability or uncertainty or tumult for any number of reasons—mostly financial ones. It's hard to keep something like that open for very long in Birmingham. The city can be really hard on all-ages venues. [Cave 9's] most notable quality was that it was present and involved and as active as it was for so long."

Lee Bains III and the Glory Fires. *Photo by Josh Weichman.*

Sometimes, it seemed being a punk rock kid in Alabama may have been more difficult than being a punk rock kid anywhere because even kids at the punk rock shows were into football. "The hardcore kids were jocks and then there were the punk kids," said producer and current owner of the Forge Matt Whitson. Whitson also fronts Birmingham's Fake Tyrants.

Though every scene has its cliques, this one was respectful. The skinheads who had caused division in the '90s were gone, and there was much less trouble to be found. Everyone was just looking for a rock show. Outsiders manufactured a lot of ideas about what was happening within the scene that were almost entirely unfounded.

"There were kids taking out their aggression in a positive manner," said Parsons. "Regardless of what type of hardcore it is, there's going to be aggression. It's aggressive music. There has always been a crowd in Birmingham that seems to have a problem with stage diving or moshing at shows, and it's like—this is punk rock. You aren't going to an acoustic coffeehouse show. I don't walk into a show wanting to be punched in the face, but when I was growing up and going to shows, I expected an element of danger. That's not always a negative thing. Jocks were the people I got into the scene to get away from."

Parsons was the resident expert on that hardcore scene. "Mike had his finger on the pulse of what kids wanted, and he knew how to book those bands and how to promote those shows and how to get kids to come out," said Thomas.

"There were the hardcore kids, mostly made up of kids who grew up Over the Mountain," said Butler. "They'd frequent the shows Mike Parsons booked but also showed up in force to support the Ackleys, and lots of them became important parts of the Cave 9 'crew.' Then there were the metalcore kids, who tended to come from northern Shelby County. There was a scene of mostly Homewood people that showed out for shows by tangentially Christian bands like Pedro the Lion. But everyone cross-pollinated, and I think that was part of what made Cave 9 different than what we've seen lately, where genres seem to be a bit more segregated."

"In high school, we were the weirdos," said Waxhatachee's Katie Crutchfield. "We were the ones that got picked on and made fun of. In a certain sense, once we started going to Cave 9, nobody at our school could really touch us. It gave us this sense of community, and it made everybody feel like people cared about them. It took everybody who was weird and into music and art and stuff. It took you from being the outsider to feeling like you were inside of something."

Cave 9 was the first time that community of young people was fully realized. It was the first real stage that a lot of those kids played on. And while there were others before and others after, it was vital to helping Birmingham find its identity.

"This place was for everyone," said Michael Shackleford of Future Elevators, formerly of the Grenadines. "People would stand outside and talk about the shows, skate, make new friends, and the ones that were old enough were usually drinking beer or liquor from solo cups. It was as punk rock as anything you'd hear about CBGB or the Chucker, but it wasn't limited to being twenty-one and up. There was always a more youthful, edgy, free-spirited element that can only authentically be portrayed through including that crowd."

Cave 9's most enduring legacy will be rooting out the punk rock kids who left town and got distribution deals with well-respected labels and toured both coasts—the Crutchfield sisters, Lee Bains III, the Grenadines and the pieces that became Wray, Future Elevators and St. Paul and the Broken Bones.

"It was really lonely," Katie Crutchfield recalls of life before Cave 9's opening. "Allison [Crutchfield, her twin sister] and I didn't really have any friends before we started playing shows at Cave 9. It's funny because a lot of the people that we ended up being friends with were also people that went to our school [Oak Mountain High School] that also played in bands and went to Cave 9. It was isolating, and it felt like there was no common ground.

"When you're that age and you're insecure and you're doing something creative—maybe deep within you, you think, 'This is cool, maybe somebody will like this!' there's always that voice in the back of your head that thinks, 'Nobody is going to like this. Nobody thinks that this is cool.' Cave 9 broke that ice for a lot of young people. It gave people a place to freely express what they were doing. It was such a good medium for that—I hate to say it was 'cutting your teeth' because it's not like everyone was gunning for success in a traditional sense—but it was a really great place for you to just forget about that weird insecurity. It attracted people that wanted to make music and people that wanted to hear music."

If we're being technical, Cave 9 was the third show that the Crutchfield sisters played. First, there was a house party where they performed five songs, and then there was a performance at the Fifth Quarter—a chaperoned Friday night postgame gathering at a church. Still, if it wasn't for their third performance—the one at Cave 9—and Hamilton's encouragement, neither may have realized their own potential and pursued the careers they now enjoy.

Their band was the Ackleys, and they shared the Fifth Quarter bill with Cinnamon Oblivion (Brad Lightfoot and Carter Wilson). Wilson encouraged the Ackleys to join them for a show at Cave 9—an eclectic bill that included around five bands for five bucks. That's when Hamilton saw the band and decided that they needed to record. It was 2004. The Crutchfields were fifteen years old.

"They had a connection to that music, and you could tell they weren't just doing it for fun," said Hamilton. "There were other people that played great music, but you could tell they weren't as invested." So, he sent them to Matt Whitson, who had his own rock bands—notably Fake Tyrants—and award-winning production projects like *We Have Signal* and *Subcarrier*, which can be seen on Alabama Public Television.

"I felt like it would be me nursing high school kids through a…demo," Whitson said, "but it turned out to be a fantastic record."

Hamilton recalls that the demo sold around one hundred copies. It led to the first P.S. Eliot record, which led to Waxahatchee and Swearin'. "The first P.S. Eliot record was actually recorded at Allison's house in Tuscaloosa during the Iron Bowl," Whitson said. "After we recorded it, we went to a succession of crazier and crazier parties."

Cave 9 was do-it-yourself, so much so that the first show was a fundraiser to buy the venue a PA system. The room would host Hopes Fall, and the promoter talked the band into playing two sets because the demand was so high. Against Me! played a set there before moving on to much larger clubs.

"We just wanted to create a warm, welcoming space for these kids, and that's how you ended up with the Ackleys and This Day Will Burn," said Thomas.

They had too much heart, as their motto proclaimed. No one was a passive part of the Cave 9 scene. The group that sustained it for six years and a day literally wore it on their sleeves. (Several have tattoos of that motto today.)

"I think the big difference is the heart," former board of directors member Renee Clay told Joey Brown in the 2007 mini documentary *We Have Too Much Heart*. "Our friends O Pioneers!!! have a lyric that says, 'We've got too much heart,' and that kind of sums it up for Cave 9. We care. We care about the music. We care about the bands that come through. We care about the kids that come to Cave 9. That's all that's kept us open. We've definitely lost a lot of our own money to take care of bands because we care."

"There's more to it than showing up and paying your money and being a spectator," said Parsons. "If that's what you did, it wasn't any different than going to a concert. There's a huge distinction between going to a show and going to a concert."

While the club's legacy is carried by the scene that it left behind and the young musicians who it influenced, its most important work is often forgotten and was the unsympathetic cause of its eventual demise.

In 2006, Cave 9 Music and Arts Project Inc. officially became a nonprofit. The venue and the community that supported it had already been assisting kids in the Magic City with tutoring and trade classes, and through its newfound legitimacy, it partnered with Scrollworks to allow kids a space to learn how to play music.

There was red tape, which is difficult to manage when no one is making any money. News quickly spread of the venue's imminent demise when Hamilton was audited, and even people from outside of the insulated community reached out with aid.

"A woman sent in a $25 donation on PayPal," Clay said in *We Have Too Much Heart*. "She had seen a story in the *Birmingham News*. Her note said, "I'm a middle-aged woman who has never been to Cave 9 and will never go to Cave 9, but I drive by and see the kids outside, and they need a place like that. So here's $25. I hope it helps."

But the bills continued to mount, and the audit was the death knell that forced the scene to migrate elsewhere. And it did. The scene moved to Firehouse and the Forge and the other house shows and clubs that will carry

Birmingham's DIY scene for many years after this one is gone. But there was something different about Cave 9—a legacy that went beyond the music, which that Hamilton carries with him today.

"Cave 9 was totally unpretentious in a way that Unity never was," said Whitson. "The group of people that surrounded Cave 9 fostered that."

Lee Bains recalls that his first trip to Cave 9 was with his band, the Shut-Ins. He also recalls that he grew to know his wife at the same club. "I went to school in New York, which is so potentially overwhelming for a kid from Birmingham," Bains said. "But I felt like I was already a part of the cultural conversation thanks to Aaron. I didn't see anything in New York that shocked me because I spent a couple of years at Cave 9. I felt like the world and its culture had been brought to us."

Hamilton was just twenty-six years old when he opened the club. The physical space certainly allowed kids to see things they'd never seen, but Hamilton's guidance and mentorship were the indelible mark he left on a scene that now represents the Magic City from coast to coast and from the City of Brotherly Love to the ATL.

"All of the friends that I made," Hamilton cites the most important thing that he took from his time at Cave 9, "there are people to this day that I love dearly and keep as friends. It was a day-by-day thing at the time where we were just trying to do something good for people—to put on a good show and to give someone some information about something that may be useful to them. Looking back, we must have made some sort of impact."

15

BOTTLETREE

On March 3, 2006, Elf Power, from Athens, Georgia, was the first band to play BottleTree Café at 3719 Third Avenue South. Nothing was in Avondale in 2006, except Parkside, which was also young. Hunter and Coby Lake didn't purchase the surrounding properties that would be anchored by Avondale Brewing Company until 2011. People didn't have any reason to go to Avondale.

The space where BottleTree was located was a tractor repair shop in the '60s, and at some point, it became a concession of gay bars. When Merrilee Challiss's parents purchased the space, it was an antiques store.

"I always knew that Avondale would turn out to be something huge," said Challiss. "I saw those empty buildings, and I saw the possibility. It's so close to the city, and it had so many great features. Logistically, it was hard because no one wanted to come to Avondale because they were scared. So, we paid extra money to have parking lots in the adjacent lot. We paid money for security. We went above and beyond as much as we could to make it welcoming and safe. We were trying to convince people to come to the industrial, desolate part of town, so we had to do things to make people feel safer."

Challiss always wanted to own her own business. She wanted a multipurpose space to house music, art, film and food. "Let's do the things we love and fill the niche of what we felt wasn't happening in Birmingham at that time," said Challiss.

She had left for a solo journey to Canada on September 10, 2001, timing that resulted in a trip filled with reflection. She saw Casa del Popola in Montreal—a place that "you could tell was done on the cheap, but it had heart." For a moment, she considered staying, and she applied to massage therapy school. But when she returned to the States, she met Brian Teasley and, within four years, decided to open a bohemian rock club on the wrong side of the tracks.

They visited the Doug Fir Lounge in Portland—a place she could tell had invested millions of dollars in the operation. She mortgaged her house, and she and her brother, Brad, got bank loans. With Teasley's help, they began booking many of the same acts as the Doug Fir Lounge on a shoestring budget and without a connected hotel. BottleTree's green room was famously two Airstream trailers behind the venue.

For eight months, BottleTree operated as a bring-your-own-beer club. Patrons were allowed to keep their beer in coolers behind the "bar," and "bartenders" would serve it to them, working for tips only. The club held nearly three hundred people—if we're being extremely generous.

Over the next nine years, Birmingham's peak DIY space hosted Vampire Weekend, the xx, alt-J, Polyphonic Spree, Dawes, the Hold Steady, Jason Isbell and the 400 Unit, Ingrid Michaelson, TV on the Radio, St. Vincent, Alabama Shakes, St. Paul and the Broken Bones and Leon Bridges, among others too numerous to name. Zach Galifianakis, Patton Oswalt and Rob Delaney performed standup there.

But BottleTree's lasting influence on the Magic City won't be the massive acts it booked, and it won't even be Challiss's decision to open a club in Avondale when no one else would. BottleTree's legacy will be unifying Birmingham's two sounds—the mainstream and the underground. It was the most inclusive space that Birmingham had seen, and it allowed local, aspiring talent a stage to play—often opening for huge acts in front of eyes that would otherwise never see their performances.

"BottleTree was definitely a unifier," Challiss said. "We tried to be. And we tried to let it be a platform for all kinds of people and all kinds of music. We got criticized for it, and it was also our strength. The thing I hate in the art world is snobbery, and I hate that in music too. When we got criticized for being 'hip indie rock,' it pissed me off. It's not what I represent or what BottleTree represented."

BottleTree is where St. Paul and the Broken Bones met and formed, and there's nothing more mainstream than that. Since then, the band has sold out weekend runs at the Alabama Theater, a venue that holds approximately 2,500.

"I think part of what BottleTree did so well was that it merged those two worlds [mainstream and underground] a little bit," said St. Paul and the Broken Bones guitarist Jesse Phillips. "Probably not something as poppy as Telluride or Brother Cane, but it had the best of both worlds. It had a DIY vibe, and it was small enough that bands from that scene could play there, and it felt good. These days, bands that play venues like Firehouse seem to exist in a different sphere than us, but I feel like when BottleTree was open, everything was passing through there."

Every band had a chance to play BottleTree's stage. Every idea was heard. Every pitch was answered.

"We always wrote people back," said Challiss. "I butted heads with people. I told them not to be a fucking snob. I wrote people back that I knew would never have a chance to play BottleTree because you should be respectful of everybody that wants to play. I tried to give everyone a chance and a platform. We ended up being the place for everybody's fundraisers. People in other venues charged organizations money to rent their spaces, but we pretty much let anybody in if they had a good idea."

BottleTree found unique ways to exist in the space between shows. There were trivia nights and Kids Got the Disco dance parties. There were film screenings and the on-again-off-again restaurant that featured the Viking Funeral (sweet potato fries covered with pimento cheese and vegan chili).

The most memorable shows at BottleTree usually came from acts that would have otherwise never existed in a Birmingham space—bands like Israeli punk rockers Monotonix, who led concertgoers into the streets of Third Avenue South and set trash on fire; Art Brut, who donned sumo wrestling costumes and grappled with one another; (!!!), who danced on top

Early St. Paul and the Broken Bones performance at BottleTree. *Photo by Jesse Phillips.*

of the bar; and David Mayfield Parade, who sat cross-legged in the center of the floor and played acoustically.

Every generation of Birmingham's scene had its own space and its own moment in time, but Bottle Tree's time overlapped with the most important time in the Magic City's growth—not just its music scene but also its urban revitalization. Merrilee and Brad Challiss are as much to credit for leading that movement as anyone, but Merrilee shies away from that today, as she did then.

"I don't own the story," said Challiss. "Everybody has their own story. It's this fractal crystalline multifaceted orb. Everyone is entitled to their own experience and what happened and what it meant to them. I felt like I was in the background. I was the den mother. Really, I was just wrangling a bunch of boys. I did payroll. I did taxes. I did the booking. I probably did every job except for running sound. I was the bartender. I worked the kitchen. I cleaned the toilets. What bar owner does that?"

16

THE GRENADINES

The Grenadines could have been Birmingham's most successful band if everyone had fully invested. But it was always sort of a side project for everyone, so it became most of Birmingham's new scene.

Lauren Strain grew up in Athens, Alabama (home of the Alabama Shakes and Anderson East), before furthering her education at the University of Alabama. She settled in Birmingham, as her then-boyfriend Matt Patton, now of Drive-By Truckers, lived there, and it was fairly close to home. That's when she decided that she wanted to start a band, but as a newcomer to town, she was disconnected from the scene—however fractured it was at the time.

John David Wheelock was the first guitarist who she recruited after seeing him play at the Nick. In 2005, they began writing songs together. Wheelock recruited Macey Taylor on keyboard, Denise Hausen (formerly of the Kidneys) on bass and John Cook on rhythm guitar. Others came and went, but that was the original core. When John David moved to New York, Michael Shackelford, from the Rewinds, joined the band.

The Rewinds—which had been All Tomorrow's Parties—had toured and released a record on LiveWire in 2006. Shackelford was the last to join the original trio of Glenn Drennan, Chris Markham and Brooks Marks, and he began writing some of their songs.

"I went from playing in a high school band, where I was playing drums and kind of starting to write some songs for this band that had already gotten a little bit of a name for themselves in the Southeast," said Shackelford. "They asked me to come play guitar. They didn't know that I was a writer.

They asked me to play a couple of tunes—they liked them—then stuck me as their lead singer all of a sudden, which I wasn't expecting. We ended up getting signed shortly after."

His high school band—named Shelton, from the middle name of bassist David Shelton Parsons—had played a couple of shows at the Hippodrome, the Rocking Horse and the Nick. That's when the Rewinds asked him to join. He toured with the band for as many as 250 dates a year for two to three years.

"A mutual friend of mine had played with him in the Rewinds, and they suggested him," said Strain of Shackelford, "so I invited him over to play and said, 'Yep. Sounds good!' He started cowriting songs with me later."

That mutual friend was Brooks Marks, who would be a drummer for the Grenadines, the drummer of Strain's most recent project Lolly and the Pops and her brother-in-law. Shackelford started writing new material shortly after joining the band.

"He actually had a demo from one of the first times that we practiced," Strain said. "He was playing at practice, and I recorded it. I later went home—not knowing that he had written a song. I think he'd actually written it for the Rewinds, but I didn't know that—and I had it on my four-track. But it didn't have lyrics or anything, so I just assumed that he'd want to work on that song. I wrote lyrics to it and recorded it and it became 'Look Around.'"

Within a couple of weeks, Strain knew she had found the right fit for her vision of what she wanted to create. "When I started, I was cowriting with Lauren, but we were working up some of the tunes they already had [with Wheelock]," said Shackelford. "And I thought, 'Isn't that kind of a weird gray area? Playing this guy's songs when he isn't in the band anymore?' So, I suggested that we do some new ones. I brainstormed some riffs and saw what stuck and what she liked, and we went from there."

Macey Taylor continued on with the new version of the Grenadines, but he had begun touring with his sister, Maria, and Conor Oberst, so he wasn't always available.

Shackelford and Strain were married in 2007.

David Swatzell worked at BottleTree, and he'd once told Strain, "If you need a guitar player, let me know." He'd been in some bands around Birmingham—mtstmtn and Comrade with Scotty Lee (now of G/T). He'd briefly backed Duquette Johnston (formerly of Verbena) alongside Shackelford in the Rebel Kings. The two also backed Taylor Hollingsworth.

"Michael called one day and said we need a guitar player for the Jenny Lewis show," said Swatzell of his first performance with the Grenadines.

"And it's the day after tomorrow. It was at the 40 Watt [Athens, Georgia]. They had sold out the Georgia Theatre, but they got a call on the way that the theater had burned to the ground, and they had to move the show."

Jesse Phillips recalls the moment that he began playing with the Grenadines differently than the version that Strain and Shackelford recall, though in both versions, he was playing bass with Secret Dangers—a band fronted by Paul Janeway (current lead singer of St. Paul and the Broken Bones). Shackelford described Secret Dangers as Led Zeppelin riffs with Janeway singing lead.

"I thought it was pretty great, personally," Shackelford said. "But it wasn't blowing anybody's minds yet until they started doing the soulful stuff and changed the name."

Per Phillips's recollection, it began with a Secret Dangers show at BottleTree, where Swatzell worked. Swatzell mentioned to Phillips that the Grenadines were playing a show in Atlanta that Friday, and they needed a bass player, so he volunteered, and they had a great set at the Earl.

"I guess at that point, I was just sort of in the band," Phillips joked. "There was no real formal invitation, as there's often not in these circumstances."

In Strain's version, she and Shackelford had seen Jesse Phillips playing a Secret Dangers show at Egan's in Tuscaloosa. Shackelford and Strain liked Phillips's sound and asked him to join the band after some confusion.

"I asked the wrong guy first," said Shackelford. "I asked somebody to ask for me because they said they were gonna see him sooner. They asked the wrong guy. They asked this guy named Dave, who was a good player and everything, but he wasn't the guy I wanted. So that was awkward. We got through a whole practice, and it was like, 'Yeah, he's nice and that was good, but I wanted to see what it'd be like with *that* guy in the mix. Eventually we got the right guy."

In either case, Secret Dangers was waning and eventually dissolved, and Phillips played bass for the Grenadines from 2009 until 2011.

"Paul [Janeway] will tell you now that I abandoned him for the Grenadines," said Phillips. "Secret Dangers was fun, but it was spinning its wheels. It never achieved a whole lot of momentum. Paul and I became close friends [while Phillips was in the Grenadines]. We'd do occasional one-off gigs at Crestwood Coffee, but those were mostly for fun."

"At some point, whoever was playing drums at the time couldn't make a run of shows," said Phillips, "so I was sitting beside the fill-in drummer—Andrew Lee—in the van." Lee would become the drummer for St. Paul and the Broken Bones.

The Grenadines first trekked to South by Southwest in 2009 for a Birmingham showcase hosted by Travis Morgan of Birmingham's Skybucket Records and Jeff Tenner of Soca Clothing. That showcase also featured Hollingsworth, 13ghosts, Through the Sparks, Kate Taylor Band, Johnston, Vulture Whale (with Wes McDonald and Les Nuby) and O+S. Jeffrey Cain, who was beginning his Birmingham-based label Communicating Vessels, dropped by the 2011 showcase. That's when he invited the Grenadines to visit his studio when they all returned. That session produced "Shake."

Cain debuted the label with a series of 7-inch releases that included "Shake" and a B side, "Colourblind." That series also included a solo release from Preston Lovinggood of Wild Sweet Orange and hip-hop act the Green Seed. A later release from Duquette Johnston included Shackelford and Swatzell as part of his backing band, the Rebel Kings. That band also included Greg Slamen on bass (Through the Sparks, formerly of Cosmonaut on Vacation) and occasionally Heath Green (Heath Green and the Makeshifters, formerly of FisherGreen) and Jody Nelson (Heath Green and the Makeshifters, Through the Sparks).

They recorded with Lynn Bridges (Devendra Banhart, Immortal Lee County Killers, Dexateens; Jim Eno, Spoon; and Andy LeMaster, Bright Eyes, Conor Oberst). They opened—alongside Dead Fingers—a tour for Maria Taylor. Macey Taylor invited Swatzell and Shackelford to play with him and his sister at one point.

"There was a point where I was playing with, like, five local bands," said Shackelford. "I played with Through the Sparks for a while. I recorded with them on *Lazarus*. There was the stuff with Duquette, Taylor Hollingsworth. At one point, he and I were joking about a project called Orange Sunglasses."

Shackelford and Strain divorced in 2013. The last Grenadines show was at Cahaba Brewing Company. It was Strain, Shackelford, Macey Taylor and Zach Evans.

"It was too difficult to continue working," said Shackelford. "You give something your all, and you try for years. And when you decide you don't have anything in you anymore, you still try to give it another year or so just to make sure that feeling doesn't change and that it's not somehow salvageable. Maybe it was bad timing. Maybe it was just young people rushing into things with big dreams and plans and the pressures of life making functionality more difficult."

On that tour with Taylor, Shackelford and Swatzell were writing some new material. Swatzell's songs became Wray songs, and Shackelford's songs became Future Elevators songs. Strain chose not to hire another guitarist.

"I guess I could have kept it going, but I felt like it would have been a different band at that point," Strain said, "and I wasn't really in the headspace to do music for a while.

"I feel like a lot of artists are great individually in their own kitchen—without getting in the same kitchen," said Shackelford. "Everybody seemed to be destined for other things. It worked out."

After the breakup, the Grenadines had its first song licensed for television. Written and arranged by Shackelford, "Down" was used in the HBO series *The Newsroom*, which stars Jeff Daniels.

"No one had even legally registered their names yet," said Shackelford. "No one was registered with ASCAP or BMI except for me—I was registered with ASCAP. And I thought that they deserved a cut. We all put a lot of time into it; we worked really hard."

It was a nice parting gift for everyone—a memorial plaque for a special project. It allowed them to recoup many of their expenses, and it allowed Shackelford to get Future Elevators off the ground.

"Over the last year or two, I had written stuff," said Shackelford. "I had written a bunch of tunes that I didn't think fit within the Grenadines and decided that was the best time to try to realize that desire to bring something that was mine back. 'Modern World' was written while I was in the Grenadines. It didn't resonate with them, and I don't know why. But it ended up being the most popular one on the Future Elevators record. Things happen for a reason."

Swatzell helped Shackelford begin Future Elevators before beginning Wray with David Brown and Blake Wimberly. The most recent version of Future Elevators was Shackelford, Ramy Noureddini, Bobby Wason (formerly with Matt Devine) and Brett Huffman. Shackelford then moved

St. Paul and the Broken Bones performing at Secret Stages in Birmingham. *Photo by Jesse Phillips.*

on to a project with his current wife, Ashley Windsor Shackelford, called Galactic Engineers of Magnetic Sounds (GEMS).

Lolly and the Pops is Strain's most recent return to music. Backed by Taylor, Swatzell, her sister Louisa and Marks, early tracks have been recorded at Communicating Vessels and Ol Elegante with Daniel Farris. Strain writes the songs.

"I was tired of drama, and I decided that these are all people that I love, and I just want to have fun," Strain said. "I've played with Brooks and David and Macey forever and ever and ever."

Jesse Phillips met former Jason Isbell and the 400 Unit guitarist Browan Lollar when the Grenadines were opening for Maria Taylor. Lollar was playing guitar in her band. When Lollar met Allison, the woman who became his wife, and decided to move to Birmingham, he gave Phillips a call.

"He asked if I would come play bass with him at some solo gigs that he had," said Phillips. "And I said, 'Yes, if you'll come play a couple of guitar parts on this recording I'm making with my friend Paul. And that turned out to be the first St. Paul and the Broken Bones EP. We recorded it at Ol Elegante with Les Nuby."

It was a chance encounter with Nuby at Birmingham's music discovery festival Secret Stages that led to the recording.

"The Grenadines were one of the main bands playing the outdoor stage at Secret Stages, and I remember running into Lester Nuby," said Phillips. "Vulture Whale was playing as well. Secret Dangers had cut a couple of demos with Lester at Ol Elegante. He asked, 'What are you and Paul up to? Are you still playing together?' I told him not much, and he sort of postulated the theory of us coming into Ol Elegante to work on some of these songs we had been working on for fun—song ideas that we had. So, we started doing that. I guess it was fall of 2011. We had some musical history together, and we thought it was a fun idea to have some sort of documentation of it."

The session began with just Phillips and Janeway. Nuby added drums—parts which remain on the EP versions of the songs.

"It was just the three of us for, like, nine months," Phillips said. "We'd go in there every week one night and spend four or five hours or whatever and throw a bunch of shit at the wall and see what stuck. Eventually, we ended up with a few things that sounded and felt like real songs. At the end of that process, we started bringing in some of the other guys. James Brangle from Through the Sparks is on that EP. We were just inviting friends in to see what we could do."

"There are all these bands—Verbena included—that were almost a household name," said Nuby. "And you fast forward to now and it's like, 'Oh, so, the band that I helped record and helped put their band together—*that's* the band?' While we were recording the first St. Paul and the Broken Bones

Right: St. Paul and the Broken Bones performing at the Alabama Theatre. *Photo by Josh Weichman.*

Below: Chad Fisher Group performs at Workplay. Chad is now the trombonist for St. Paul and the Broken Bones. *Photo by Don Naman.*

stuff, we were like, 'Man, what if this actually works? This could be cool. This is a lot of fun.' It's interesting the way the family tree of Birmingham works because right when you think the highwater mark is Remy Zero, it's like, 'Nope! St. Paul and the Broken Bones.'"

Phillips played with both bands in 2012. But the St. Paul and the Broken Bones calendar began to fill, and he soon found himself missing too many shows with the Grenadines. He phased out of the Grenadines and focused all of his efforts on the new project.

"The Grenadines had scheduled a solid summer tour at some point that conflicted with some St. Paul stuff that I had," said Phillips. "I had been missing a lot of work too. I had to tell them that I couldn't do the tour."

It was never an official exit. That's never been the way these things work. The relationship just drifted away. "When we started St. Paul and the Broken Bones, the goal was to sell out BottleTree," said Phillips. "And when that started happening, it felt like a raging success already. That was our measure of success."

17

FIREHOUSE

As soon as Homewood native Eric Wallace was old enough to drive, he was going to DIY shows across metro Birmingham. From the west side down to Montevallo's Barnstormer's, these were shows in old warehouses to new pizza joints. DIY Birmingham is something that became part of his identity at an early age, and it's something that he continues supporting—rather quietly—nearly two decades later.

"When it becomes a part of your life for longer than it hasn't been a part of your life, then it's just sort of what you do," Wallace said. "It happened to work out that I was able to provide a space, and it was awesome. And like all DIY spaces, it won't be here forever, but it's really cool while it is here."

That space is a historic firehouse that Wallace purchased in the then largely forgotten and abandoned east Birmingham community of Avondale. He purchased this building in 2009—a couple of years before Coby and Hunter Lake opened Avondale Brewing Company down the street. Wallace had only one real neighbor in the now-revitalized Birmingham neighborhood— BottleTree Café. BottleTree has since been home to Saigon Noodle House and is now Rodney Scott's BBQ, and the Lake brothers no longer own Avondale Brewing Company.

"After I left college, like most people in touring bands, I was working in restaurants, making it work while you're at home so you can make it work while you're out on the road," Wallace said. "I had begun teaching guitar on the side, and the dream became having a place where I could live, have a studio, where I could teach and, hopefully, do something like have a space where I could let people put on DIY shows."

Firehouse. *Author's photo.*

But people weren't moving to Avondale to do things like that in 2009. At least, no one had done so other than Brian Teasley and Merrilee Challiss.

"I kind of liked the fact that nobody was there," said Wallace. "I've always been interested in repurposing old things. When I was in college, I had interned for a city planner, so I was constantly immersed in the goings-on of downtown Birmingham, and I was always reading about the city's history. It was just sort of a no-brainer for me."

Nearly a decade later, Avondale is one of the city's hippest entertainment districts. Folks like Paget Pizitz have opened Melt, Fancy's on Fifth and the Marble Ring. Tom Bagby opened an ode to the classic Birmingham hot dog called Hot Diggity Dogs. The second location of Saw's BBQ is just down the street, and several other bars and restaurants call the Forty-First Street area home.

Like so many others from his generation, Wallace was inspired by Cave 9 and Aaron Hamilton. "It wasn't just the ability to have a space to keep the music alive, but he was an iconic dude and he knew who everybody was," said Wallace of Hamilton. "I remember one year—I think I turned nineteen—and he sent me a text on my birthday, and I thought, 'Oh man! How cool!' I still think about it. I've made a pretty good run at being a musician here for most of my life, and if my shitty bands hadn't had a place to legitimize our art-making when I was that age, I don't think that would be the case."

Wallace recalls that the first band he played with at Cave 9 was Salesmen, but he can't remember when they played or who was on the bill.

When he moved to Avodale, Cave 9's demise was in its latter stages, and BottleTree was growing rapidly. A void was emerging for another stage, and the space that he had purchased seemed viable.

"When it started out, it was really just my bands practicing there," Wallace, formerly of the Monitors and Wildcat Revival, said. "And somewhere in that first year, between Cave 9 closing and a show needing to happen that couldn't go on at BottleTree, somebody approached me and said, 'Can we just do it there?' And it was like, 'Yeah. Sure. Let's do that.'"

It was unceremonious, unmemorable, in Wallace's own words. He can't remember who played that first show either. It just happened, and that is and was the heart of Birmingham's DIY scene.

"It was probably glorified band practices, to be honest," he said, "and that may be how the last show is."

Like every DIY space that came before it, Firehouse is more for the scene than the owner. But Firehouse has an advantage over all of its notable DIY predecessors, as Wallace purchased the property long before the Avondale community's property values skyrocketed, and he still lives there. As long as he does, there's no real overhead.

"Nobody that has anything to do with putting on DIY shows has ever made a single dime," he said. "Nobody can spend their whole life doing it because it takes more than a lifetime of energy to support art forms that don't make a lot of money. However, it's so utterly necessary to have a place within the community where that sort of thing can go on and the bottom line isn't an issue.

It's just a space. There's no bar. There are four walls and a couple of microphones. It's all ages. There's no website or Facebook or Twitter or Instagram. It's the type of space where young bands play in front of people for the first time, and they spread the word the old-fashioned way—word of mouth. Sure, that can be an email newsletter now, but it's also still fliers.

That's right—fliers. Often, venues at the next level up—the venue with the bar and the sound guy and light crew—think promotion can be as simple as creating a Facebook event page. But the DIY scene in Birmingham still relies on old-fashioned show promotion.

The Frequently performing at Firehouse. *Photo by Jones Willingham.*

Now a guitarist for Lee Bains III and the Glory Fires, weeks can go by with Wallace on tour and unable to tend to the space. But the community that has been built over the past three decades remains as reliable and committed as they ever have.

"DIY Birmingham is run by some really, really awesome people," he said. "When I'm on tour, the place is always in good hands. There really is a super solid community of folks that takes care of the place."

Firehouse will remain an art space for the community that it quietly helped reinvigorate for the foreseeable future. "The beauty of having an art space is that there doesn't have to be a beginning and an end planned," Wallace said. "I feel like these things have always happened organically, and as long as everybody's ego stays out of it, then they keep going, or they may lead to other places."

And the scene will remain beyond Firehouse, as it did beyond Bubba Town, the Tuxedo Junction Ballroom, Unity and Cave 9.

"The people of Birmingham are very protective of their community and they realize the value of being able to make art within it," Wallace said. "Flag waving is much less important to me than actually doing those things because there are so many people that are looking to capitalize on what you do and where you're from.

18

TAYLOR

Macey Taylor Sr. grew up in Homewood, Alabama, one of the closest suburbs to Birmingham's city center, and he spent his entire youth around music. His mom, Veronica, spun a lot of Glenn Miller records, and his older siblings introduced him to Elvis Presley. Once, his older brother Bobby had a friend named Joe who played guitar, and Joe worked hard to teach Bobby a lick as Macey looked on, but he couldn't get it. The older boys left the room, and Macey picked up the guitar that had been left behind and nailed it. Excited that he was able to catch on so quickly—and even more excited that he had accomplished something that his brother couldn't—Macey stormed downstairs and showed his new trick to his mom. He had the bug.

He got his first guitar in 1963. He still has it today. He was lent his first electric later that summer—a Les Paul Jr. He was pretty bummed out when he had to return that one twenty years later.

A couple of his friends from school recruited him to play in their band, the Dirt Daubers. Taylor played some college parties with that band for a couple of years before it fizzled out. And he had a few bands that fizzled out before they ever got off the ground, as bands often do.

In the late '60s, there weren't many clubs to see live music. There were some young band showcases at Eastwood Mall and downtown at the Pizitz. They got their rock-and-roll fix at local armories—the Oporto and the Airport—local radio stations would host shows there. Occasionally, a big regional act would pass through and join the bill.

Taylor and his peers were among the first who craved the art and knew that they had to go downtown to get it. Young and white, they were among the minority when they visited downtown Birmingham's Boutwell Auditorium to see the likes of James Brown and Otis Redding during the city's most challenging years.

When he was in the navy, Taylor jammed with lounge acts all over the world. Once, he hopped on stage at a spot in Iran and introduced the audience to American R&B. When he returned, he formed a duo and played clubs around Birmingham.

Throughout his adult life, Taylor wrote jingles for local companies. Notably, he wrote the jingle for Milo's Hamburgers—"Everybody goes to Milo's." He recorded advertising music for Birmingham-based businesses like Regions Bank and Zeigler's and Barber's, and he had one national jingle for Blimpie's, "Simply Blimpie."

"A lot of times when I listen to my old stuff, I'll forget I did it all," Taylor joked. "It's like, 'Damn. Who did that?'"

Taylor and his then-wife, Pat, had their first daughter, Maria, in 1976, and Macey left the band he was in at the time. He started doing session work. When Maria was a toddler, she had a play castle and a toy piano, and she came to call it *her* studio. She grabbed her dad's recorder and began recording songs of her own.

Macey had cowritten a song called "Beat the Clock." Maria was six years old, and as a background singer, she got her first studio work as a background vocalist on that demo. That recording happened in the home studio of Mark Harrelson shortly before he began a three-decade career as the engineer at Boutwell Studios.

Maria spent most of her teen years in ballet before meeting Orenda Fink in high school at Alabama School of Fine Arts. The pair formed Little Red Rocket, which was signed to Geffen Records, before moving to Athens, Georgia, where they evolved in Azure Ray, which signed to Saddle Creek Records.

Maria struck out on her own with her solo debut *11:11* in 2005.

Macey Taylor Jr. was his father's second child. The younger Taylor went to Homewood High School, and by this time, the elder had gotten into a groove with studio and production work.

The younger Taylor found his own way. When he was in second grade, his father bought him a miniature Fender Stratocaster. He still has it today. His dad taught him the same licks he learned from his brother as a kid, some Chuck Berry. Taylor took his two licks and his guitar and amp to show-and-tell in his second-grade classroom.

"When he got home, he said, 'Dad, when I finished, everyone clapped,'" the elder Taylor said. "And he just had this look in his eyes. I think he was bitten right then and there."

Taylor was around his older sister a lot when she was in Little Red Rocket, and he started playing on his own around 2003. "I've often joked that I took a semester off of school in 2005 to go out on tour and that I'm still on that tour," the younger Taylor said.

He stayed busy and kept taking more jobs. He played in several Birmingham bands, including the Grenadines and Taylor Hollingsworth, and he has toured as the bassist for A.A. Bondy, Jenny Lewis, Amanda Shires, Har Mar Superstar, Bright Eyes and his sister Maria.

He spent a lot of time playing with Conor Oberst in various projects, including Conor Oberst and the Mystic Valley Band, which also included Hollingsworth. And he still finds time to jam with Birmingham musicians and friends when he's not on the road.

The youngest Taylor, Kate, found her way into music after high school. She had played around at local coffee shops, but the time she spent hanging with her friends in Wild Sweet Orange was when she began taking it a little more seriously. She started playing shows in the Edgewood community of Homewood at Cool Beans Coffee House, where she was working at the time.

That's the same time Maria decided to record *11:11*. Kate was nineteen, and she and her brother hit the road with their sister.

"That's when I really started touring a lot," Kate said. "Traveling and getting out on the road, getting my feet wet. I think I turned twenty when I was on tour. And it was pretty heavy touring. I think that first tour was seven straight weeks, then we had four days off and went to Europe for a couple of weeks, then we came back for a couple of weeks and got back out on the road in the United States. It was the best. At that time, I had no doubt that I was doing what I loved. And to share that with my brother and sister was really great."

She first met Taylor Hollingsworth when the two were working at Rojo, a restaurant in Birmingham's Highland Park community. They became close friends and started playing music together. Eventually, Hollingsworth joined Maria on tour.

"When we were out on the road, those lines of friendship started to get a little blurry," Kate joked. "I think we were on tour when we realized that we were fooling ourselves, trying to pretend that it wasn't something. We came home from that tour and moved in together."

Dead Fingers. *Courtesy of Dead Fingers Facebook page.*

The two began recording and performing as Dead Fingers. Hollingsworth played most of Kate's shows with her when he wasn't on tour with Conor Oberst and the Mystic Valley Band, and it eventually evolved into a duo project.

"It was just us putting stuff together, playing stuff in our living room, sitting on our couch, and we just kind of started doing that on stage," Kate said. "We'd play a Tom Petty cover and a Chuck Berry cover—just piecing stuff together sitting around the house. We just had fun doing it, and then we started taking it more seriously."

Bruce Watson at Fat Possum Records in Water Valley, Mississippi, led the duo to Big Legal Mess, a subsidiary label of the former. Their second album was released on Birmingham's Communicating Vessels.

Hollingsworth performed with Flair for the first time when he was working with the other members of the band at Chesapeake Bagel (now Crestline Bagel) in the Crestline Village community of Mountain Brook. Flair broke up, and Hollingsworth joined Duquette Johnston's project Cutgrass. (Matt Patton of the Dexateens and Drive-By Truckers was also part of Cutgrass.) He also toured with Johnston in a later version of Verbena.

Tired of jumping from band to band, Hollingsworth started his own thing. It began as Taylor and the Puffs before evolving into Taylor Hollingsworth. He recorded all of the instruments on those projects, and Macey Taylor Jr. consistently joined for live performances. He spent a lot of time on the road with Oberst, and he joined the Dexateens for a second time. The first time he left, he was replaced by Lee Bains III, and upon Bains's departure, he returned. Today, he performs as Taylor Hollingsworth Country Western.

Holy Youth performing at the Syndicate Lounge. *Photo by Don Naman.*

Mark Harrelson moved all of his recording equipment to Boutwell Studios around 1983, and the place that also housed his old studio served as a storage space for many years. Kate and Taylor Hollingsworth bought the home a few years ago and gave new life to the space that once saw recordings ranging from Telluride to Jim Bob and the Leisure Suits.

"While the studio space wasn't the primary reason they bought the house, I like to think it played at least a small part," Harrelson said. "I really like the idea of music happening down there again."

Taylor Sr. played keys with Dead Fingers. He also played with the family band—a collective the Taylors and Hollingsworth got together at venues from the downtown masonic lodge to Zydeco to the Nick around Christmas each year. When Oberst and Maria were dating, he'd sit in too. Once, David Rawlings and Gillian Welch made a surprise appearance.

Maria and her husband, Ryan Dwyer, created their own label, Flower Moon Records, and its first release was Maria's 2016 album *In the Next Life.* The label has since released albums by Louis Schefano, compilations and a reunited Azure Ray.

On August 2, 2019, Taylor Hollingsworth released his latest solo effort *Tap Dancin' Daddy*, on Flower Moon.

EPILOGUE

There are countless artists and bands who were never mentioned in this book—or perhaps only briefly. There are others who appeared only speaking about some other venue or act that was important to their own growth. There are simply too many to count. And there are many more

Alabama Theatre. *Photo by Josh Weichman.*

who continue to help guide the Magic City's scene into the next decade and beyond—Will Stewart and his second project with Janet Simpson, Timber, the latest project from Verbena's Les Nuby, Holiday Gunfire, the solo works of Brad Armstrong and Preston Lovinggood, Terry Ohms, Taylor Hunnicutt, BEITTHEMEANS, Stoned Cobra, IN SNOW, NULL, Lady Legs, Dree Lear, the Burning Peppermints, the Frequently, Captain Kudzu and far too many more to name.

And in 2019, though he no longer lives in Birmingham, A.A. Bondy returned to release his first new music in eight years.

The people who built the scene—the people who actually fought people who identified as Nazis to maintain their creative city enclaves—still guide it today. Artists have come, and others have gone. But the community that has remained has grown to become a supportive one, and the future of Magic City rock is bright.

BIBLIOGRAPHY

Interviews

Bagby, Tom (promoter, business owner). In-person interview with the author, June 22, 2017.

Bains, Lee, III (musician). Telephone interview with the author, January 2017.

Bodarenko, Leif (musician). In-person interview with the author, June 9, 2017.

Boykin, Tim (musician). Telephone interview with the author, August 8, 2017.

Bunton, Jacob (musician). Email interview with the author, July 24, 2017.

Butler, Will (former concert promoter). Email interview with the author, May 2017.

Cain, Jeffrey (musician, record label owner). In-person interview with the author, December 2013.

Carter, Rick (musician). Telephone interview with the author, May 18, 2017.

Challiss, Merrilee (business owner, artist). In-person interview with the author, March 2017.

Crutchfield, Katie (musician). Telephone interview with the author, January 2017.

Flournoy, Layne (business owner). Telephone interview with the author, January 2016.

Glaze, Ed (musician). Telephone interview with the author, June 2017.

Griffin, Anne-Marie (musician). Telephone interview with the author, September 9, 2017.

Griffin, Carole (musician, business owner). In-person interview with the author, May 31, 2017.

Hamilton, Aaron (business owner). In-person interview with the author, January 2017.

Harrelson, Mark (business owner). Email interview with the author, December 2017.

Hawkins, Davis (radio executive). Telephone interview with the author, March 2017.

Holmes, Jeff (musician). Telephone interview with the author, March 2017.

Johnson, Damon (musician). Telephone interview with the author, March 2016.

Johnston, Duquette (musician, business owner). In-person interview with the author, August 23, 2017.

Mayfield, Matthew (musician). Telephone interview with the author, February 2017.

Nolen, Dan (business owner). Telephone interview with the author, February 2017.

Nuby, Les (musician). Telephone interview with the author, August 2017.

Parsons, Mike (concert promoter). In-person interview with the author, May 2017.

Pearson, Geno (radio programmer). Email interview with the author, March 2017.

Phillips, Jesse (musician). Telephone interview with the author, October 2017.

Phillips, Marc (musician). Telephone interview with the author, October 27, 2017.

Ranelli, Frank (business owner). Telephone interview with the author, November 2017.

Reaves, Rodney (musician). Telephone interview with the author, August 2017.

Register, Scott (radio personality). In-person interview with the author, March 22, 2017.

Shackelford, Michael (musician). Telephone interview with the author, October 2017.

Strain, Lauren (musician, artist). Telephone interview with the author, October 2017.

Taylor-Hollingsworth, Kate (musician). Telephone interview with the author, October 2017.

Taylor, Macey, Jr., (musician). Telephone interview with the author, October 2017.

Taylor, Macey, Sr. (musician). Telephone interview with the author, October 2017.

Thomas, Trent (former concert promoter). In-person interview with the author, January 2017.

Wallace, Eric (musician, business owner). Telephone interview with the author, November 2017.

Watters, Eric (musician). Telephone interview with the author, May 2019.

Whitson, Matt (musician, promoter). In-person interview with the author, January 2017.

Magazines

Barra, Allen. "Sweet Home Alabama: New Wave Meets Southern Hospitality." *Trouser Press*, September 1981.

Newspapers

Barra, Allen. "Leisure Suits Find Being Different Has Its Price." *Kudzu*, July 16, 1982.

Carlton, Bob. "Packing the Leisure Suits, Moving On." *Birmingham News*, February 10, 1983.

———. "Jim Bob Hangs Up Leisure Suits." *Birmingham News*, June 9, 1983.

Kemp, Kathy. "It's No Joke: Suits Are Getting Serious." *Kudzu*, April 1, 1983.

Films

Cookson, Shari, dir. *Skinheads USA*. HBO, 1993.

ABOUT THE AUTHOR

Blake Ells is a freelance writer whose work has been published in AL.com, *Birmingham Post-Herald*, *Birmingham News*, *Weld: Birmingham's Newspaper*, *Birmingham Magazine*, *Good Grit*, *Leeds Tribune* and *Over the Mountain Journal*, among many others. Blake served on the Literacy Council of Central Alabama, where he was a past chair, as well as with Alzheimer's of Central Alabama and the Alabama Symphony Orchestra. He is a proud alumnus of Auburn University and was raised in Rogersville, Alabama, but he currently resides in Birmingham. Follow him @blakeells.